CRUCIFYING
A
COLOR

CRUCIFYING

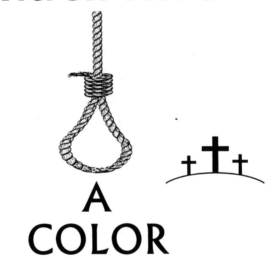

A
COLOR

KENNETH L. JOHNSON, M.A., M.Div.

**Understanding The Nature Of
Our Blackness**

HARLO   DETROIT

Copyright © 1996 by Kenneth L. Johnson

ISBN: 0-9622324-1-6
Library of Congress Catalog Card No.: 96-78186

FERTILE SOIL PUBLISHING
P.O. BOX 48066
OAK PARK,MICHIGAN 48237-5766
PHONE/FAX: (313)534-6358

Printed by Harlo Press, 50 Victor, Detroit, Michigan 48203

**In Loving Memory Of
My Father**

DEACON L.J. JOHNSON
(Long Journey Home)
December 14, 1995

CONTENTS

Preference

I dedicate this writing to my parents who struggled lovingly to protect me, my sister, and my brothers from the rejection of racism. As I recall, I would not begin to realize the scope and depth of dislike for me on account of skin color until I entered the university my freshman year. Two events remain indelibly etched in my mind, one on campus and the other off but near campus. Needless to say, I was unprepared and rudely awakened to a reality through both events that did not make such sense to me. I was being judged by my skin color.

As far back as I can remember, I loved to attended Sunday church worship service. I wanted to be close to God and saw no better place to do so than the church.

Upon attending the university, I suddenly found myself living on campus, new, and without transportation. I quickly learned that my choices of churches to attend for that very reason would be limited. I was baptist then. Knowing no difference, to me, baptist was baptist. I sought out a baptist church close by. I found a Southern Baptist Church of which the word southern meant nothing to me. I simply wanted

7

to attend church on Sunday as usual and it was close enough to walk. I did sitting on the front pew as usual. It did not matter to me that everyone else was white. After church service, I was made welcome by all who greeted me. I came away thinking white people aren't so bad. In fact, as far as I was concerned, they were alright.

I had decided this was going to be my church while I lived on campus in the dormitory. It was close by and it meant that I could get back in time for lunch, the last meal served on Sunday in the dorm cafeteria. I had little money and could not afford to miss any meals.

The next Sunday morning down the hill I walked eager to arrive at my new church when a car pulled up beside me. I looked in and recognized the driver as one of the deacons of the church. He was offering me a ride and I accepted. Now I was really convinced. These people are really nice. Then we began to converse as he drove slowly. Then the question which was very perplexing to me at that moment: "Don't you want to go to one of your own churches?" I really did not know what he meant. The question of race never even entered my mind. I thought this was a church like my own. It was baptist and that was all that mattered to me. Yet I hesistantly said yes more so out of curiosity. I wanted to know what he meant by one of my own churches.

He turned off and drove me a great distance across town to a church which I would come to understand was one of my own. Its congregation and pastor were all black. I got out of the car, thanked him, and went in. When church service ended following an extended period of time, I came out first realizing time was short before the dorm cafeteria would close. Secondly I realized that I did not know exactly where I was in relations to the campus let alone my dorm. I never made it back in time for lunch despite a desperate effort. The event was traumatic to me at the time and I never told anyone back then. I would never return to the church close by again because I felt rejection. As a result, I would continuously reflect on this experience as regarded the purpose of the church.

As the academic year got underway, I enrolled for a semester of Western Civilization, a required course of study. It was being taught by a tenured professor who I believed was head of the department. I was the only black student in his class at that hour. The class had been informed that 50% of our course grade depended on midterm results and the other 50% on the final. Upon completing the midterm examination we were instructed to use a numbering system as opposed to putting our names on the examination when turning it in. When time came to receive back our graded midterm exams, he called out the number on the exam not knowing to whom it belonged and we would respond. When he called my number which I had, I hurriedly walked up to his desk and reached over to receive my graded exam. As he went to hand it to me, he pulled back gesturing for me to lean forward. He whispered: "Had I known that this was your exam. It would not have mattered how good it was. I would have given you a F because I do not believe you should be here." I simply and politely smiled returning to my seat with the exam in hand. I slowly opened it having accepted my fate as reflected in his comment to surprisingly find a grade of an A. I was initially elated knowing that he could not fail me now no matter how he tried. This was 50% of my course grade. Then I pondered the question of whether or not to believe that he would simply recognize the writing of this one black student. Therefore he could have justiably given it a grade of F. He could easily have argued that he did not know which paper belonged to whom because he had used a number system and not names on the exams. I would not have had any recourse by which to address such an injustice. The comment: "If I had known. . .'and' I do not believe you should be here," clearly meant that he had intended to hurt my chances of remaining as a student at the university. He failed.

I was realizing what it was my parents had sought to defend me from. It was this issue of race and the racism it causes of which I became fully conscious of rather suddenly. From that point forward I have pondered on the reality of race and the ignorance of race. This writing is a conscious awakening to those issues. I opened my eyes so that I could really see.

Introduction

"Gunnar Myrdal, the Swedish sociologist, claims that racism indicates Americans' 'need for a defense. . .against their national creed.'[30] In effect, racism is intentional: it is a coherent policy that served pragmatically to expedite the functioning of the diverse industrial state by consolidating diverse Americans. It is, therefore, as DuBois saw, a 'deliberately cultivated and encouraged state of mind.'[31] Only Indians, who were progressively eliminated, and blacks have 'never been included in the original consensus universalis (universal consensus) of the American republic.'[32] Capitalistic democracy depended on the black: had he not been brought to America in the beginning of its history, he would have had to be invented. In a real sense, he was invented. Black is an abstraction which stands outside the existence of black individuals. In other words, black is a category which misrepresents the person in himself."[1]

The first humans are not to be identified using racial terminology but rather in the historical and biological context in which the first humans existed. They were a black-

11

skinned people. Even today in biological terms we are still very much black-skinned people. From the beginning humans were meant to be black-skinned. The production of melanin can be and has been altered (not intentionally but nevertheless altered) for some reducing its presence. Any human denying one's blackness is simply in a state of denial. We are all black-skinned people. While one may not appear visually to be black, closer examination of the skin, environmental awareness, and an understanding of mutagenesis saids otherwise. There is a black-skinned ancestral heritage in everyone's past. In fact if it were not for the unique set of events which took place long ago (which could occur again given the right circumstances) to be described later in this writing, this discussion on classifying individual/s basically according to skin color would be moot because black skin would be abundantly present in everyone.

Unless we invented race because of the presence of a greater or lesser amount of melanin produced in one's skin to categorize them into sub-groups for identity purposes or to socially categorize people, we are to understand that all humans are biologically black and obviously with variation thereof resulting from a not so obvious environmental impact. But then race was not invented merely as a figment of someone's imagination, was not invented from factual and unbias scientific inquiry, nor does race have a theological/religious/biblical foundation in the exegetical sense. Rather, its use can be deemed a social, psychological, political, and historical sin or a crime against humanity. The use of race in reference to humans is scientific falsification and biblical isogetics. The intent was to divide humans for purposes of socio-political-economic dominance, in summation secular greed. Several individuals, acting and reacting, have benefited greatly by distorting human history into such categories as race. For this reason, those individuals in positions of influence would taint the minds of those unwilling to see for themselves. Those unwilling to see believe and act upon the images given to them by individuals with hidden agendas. Even today the economy is in large part being race driven. Yet in human nature or in understanding human history:

"Human racial classification is of no social value and is positively destructive of social and human relations. Since such racial classification is now seen to be of virtually no genetic or taxonomic significance either, no justification can be offered for its continuance."[2]

Scientific advances have shown that diversity within a so-called race has greater significance than the diversity between two different so-called races establishing a fault and misrepresentation in our perception and socialization.

"What has changed during the evolution of scientific thought, and is still changing, is our perception of the relative importance and extent of intragroup as opposed to intergroup variation. These changes have been in part a reflection of the uncovering of new biological facts. . . They have also reflected general sociopolitical biases derived from human social experience and carried over into 'scientific' realms."[3]

Some have used their scientific credentials, wealth, or political status and skills to socially muddy the water successfully thus far in preventing most of us, black/white, from seeing that this understanding of the black/white idea of race is literally nonsensical.

Biologically it can be shown that no human has ever not with the exception of some albinos had the presence of some melanin. Melanin is the primary substance responsible for skin coloring which we all know to be a black/brown pigment.

In fact an article by P.A. Riley suggest that modifications of the skin pigmentation is not only possible but probable. Such modifications can occur as a result of mutations which this writing addresses. P.A. Riley states:

". . . There are multiple control points in the process of melanin production. . . The reactions involved account for the unusual kinetics of tyrosine oxidation and suggest biochemical mechanisms whereby the activity of the enzyme and the process of melanogenesis may be modified.

The surface pigmentation of vertebrates is mainly due to melanin.

Generally speaking the pattern of pigmentation is a reflection of the distribution of melanogenic cells and the degree of pigmentation is a function of the rate of synthesis of pigment, the type of pigment generated, and the extent of donation of the pigment to recipient cells.

. . .the most important enzyme in the melanogenic pathway is tyrosinase. In the absence of tyrosinase activity no melanin is formed. In addition to genetic modification of the enzyme, there are a number of controls that may act at various epigenetic levels such as transcription, translation, and post-translational modification of the enzyme. . .controls affecting the vesicular routing of the product, as well as mechanisms affecting the rate of aggregation of premelanosomes with coated vesicles giving rise to stage I melanosomes."[4]

As we can clearly see, we are not talking about skin color in the context of distinguishing races but skin pigmentation which begs the question of how much melanin is present and how black/brown a person might be. This is the issue to be addressed. It is not a question of what race one is.

We all are to be considered a black people or shades thereof in the biological sense and in a human sense. So it is only a question of how black. The variation of blackness depends upon the structure and functioning of the melanocytes. Alterations of these structures or their functioning can give the appearance of significant changes when in fact it has merely resulted in superficial and meaningless variations in the skin tissue most obviously the color. Such changes are the result of mutations of the genes. All living tissue is composed of genes of which some are more predisposed to change or alteration than others. The redisposition of the skin's genetic structure subjects it to changes or alterations given exposure to certain circumstances. The alteration in the functioning of those genes are caused by mutations. The mutations occur in the DNA of the gene or in the promoter. "A promoter is generally defined as a segment of DNA (usually immediately preceding a gene or genes) that contains signals for proper binding and subsequent activation of RNA polymerase holoenzyme to a form capable of initiating the synthesis of RNA."[5] Alterations or mutations can be affected by a process called ionization. Subsequently the instructional template (the DNA or the promoter) can be changed and made to give new instructions resulting in a different genetic transcription. It is this transcript which will be produced now and over again in the future. Such incidences are suspected in the pigmentation variations which improperly and inappropriately have been to date referred to as racial characteristics even though scientifically and when defining the term race we should know better.

Clearly, the institutionalization of race into a belief system precludes and excludes scientific advances and ignores unbiased academic not to mention religious teachings. The world is in desperate need of global discussions to eradicate ideas of race as communications technology brings us closer. We must discover the greater similarities over the lesser dissimilarities which have insignificant meaning. We can get it together if we are willing to try and if we are mature enough to see beyond the hate being fostered within the idea of race.

Yet the point must be made. Those of the so-called minority race specifically Black (African American) people are not looking for a new approach to integration or assimilation (themes of the civil rights era of the 1960-70s) because such systems assume and revitalizes ideas of race bringing to mind differences and images of superior/inferior. Besides what one brings to the table is not a question of skin color but one of character. Even when embracing ethnic pluralism or cultural diversity, we invent in reality new code words for race disguishing the racism within our social system. But there does need to be what I call a historogration/retrogration of human existence which is an integration of human history to understand the nature of all human blackness. This simply means an understanding of all human history as contributing to one. There is no human history to which I can not lay claim with a sense of accomplishment. After all we are each only shades of black not separate and distinct people by color. No one from the beginning to the present has succeeded without standing on the shoulders of those black-skinned ancestors even if we no longer remember any relations to the shoulders upon which we once stood.

We can not truthfully shape history in the context of the present proposed dominant image. We have in fact been in error developing a so-called European or white history and then in turn developing a so-called African American or Black history in reaction. We will find any such history to be mythical in their origin when making racial claims. While we may have become separated by migrations and isolated from one another for very prolonged periods of time long forgotten, we are still the same humans (as in one) with our hereditary development having been in response to the environmental circumstances in which they found themselves. In some instance it would result in superficial mutational changes resulting in the eye, hair, and skin variations. One's blackness can be diluted by such impacts although remaining ever present because black/brown is the only color we can be primarily with other skin colors resulting from secondary systems showing through only when the black/brown has become insufficiently present and not easily observable.

This writing is intended to explain the inappropriate and nonsensical use of race in regard to humans while cautioning the reader to the awareness of a socio-political dominance which has portrayed the world in black/white racial terminology and inventions. This is ashamedly the real world which has unfortunately been deceitful and intentionally disconnecting when presenting religious truths and/ or scientific fact on the subject of human oneness. On the matter of race, a small element of society has mounted orchestrated distortions of reality seemingly for socio-political-economic gains. Their maligned desire is to use the imagery of self around which to shape the future. Meaning, the future must not only be how they see it but it must evolve around them as well. If we consider the commercials, the news reporting, or mass media in general, we will find that they are succeeding at fooling most of the people with such imagery most of the time although not all. Many of the voices which we need to hear but have not yet heard are being presented disjoint in scientific journals and go lacking of an audience because of social conformity.

It has not been accidental but a deliberate attempt to sustain a traditional belief and to prevent an understanding of our blackness. Our consciousness of a biological blackness has become so altered and distorted that we have all but ceased searching for a more true and united human understanding which lies today scattered among all the research in bits and pieces. The conclusion reached in the accumulation of such bits and pieces of research has been a reaffirmation and a confirmation of the biological blackness in all humans. In other words the skillet can not call the kettle black because the skillet is not white but black itself having simply a variation of blackness in color resulting from radiation genetics.

In fact if we have noticed the television from its beginning to now, all things that are supposed to be good is either told by a so-called white person or approved to be said although coming out of the mouths of others through editing. Through mass communications the shaping of the future imagery has long been in effect. White is supposed to always be right. It is this image of society being portrayed in such instances as to how we are to raise children to how we are to behave in relations to one another; how we are to worship to what color is God; what is moral and acceptable and what is not to how we should view what is justice. Everything for the future is to become a reflection of their ideology and what they approve/disapprove. Clearly the intent is for everyone to be white or to act like it. Anything else is being portrayed in negative imagery. One can thus be assured that the world will self destruct when the rest of the world's people who are not classified as white totally objects.

It can be shown that many people of color have embraced the indoctrination that white people are always right without question denying even their own sense of right/ wrong. Subsequently such imagery is always given a positive spin even when proven to be clearly wrong, guilty, or distortions to truth. This is why even when committing a horrible and unspeakable crime some way is found to soften the violence of the image or to glorify it. But if one of color particularly of the so-called Black race is accused, guilt is assumed without benefit of reasonable doubt or until proven. Even when proven to be innocent, one may still be considered guilty if they do not agree. Race immediately becomes a factor. Race for those who believe themselves to always be right has always caused a rush to judgement. We are fooling ourselves if we think that the idea of race has been and is a good thing. It will forever remain a decisive tool in the hands of some because different no matter how we define it or look at it, it can never be the same. The so-called races can never be made to be equal when by the connotated definition of what folks say it means, different. We will see in this writing that we need seriously to re-evaluate the human self. Are we guilty of believing in race a term which divides people and should not even exist.

This idea of race must be eradicated from society. But it does not stop there. We must use the tools at our disposal to become desensitized to skin color and all of its ramifications in the imagery to avoid instances of reinventing the wheel under a new disguise. It will require what I have referred to as a historogration to bring this more truthful understanding of humans into our classroom, our religious preaching/teaching, our places of employment, into our social gatherings and our family conversations. We must not only expunge race and racial terminology from human relationships and human nature or development. We must extricate human understanding from the falsification of traditional and institutionalized beliefs if we are to know that despite it all, we are truly brothers and sisters. This is one point that I hope to convey. To make my point more clearly, quite naturally we will begin by looking at definitions on race to determine the irrelevance of race to human understanding and to determine the basis of its falsification and usage.

Chapter One

When was the last time any one in this technologically advancing nation and world of ours took a moment of one's time to look up one of the most disruptive and nonsensical terms in American society and indeed the whole world, race. The use of the term race can divide one against another. The term race has been the root cause of much hatred, prejudices, and bigotry. People have killed one another and indeed used the term to justify enslaving others on account of one's understanding of the term race. Inequality in education, in the job market, in housing and in society across the board exist because of the understanding by the populace of the word race regardless of gender, education, profession, or wealth and yes regardless of skin color. We have mistakenly viewed humanity through this prism of race seeing a disillusionment of ourselves.

According to the Random House Unabridged Dictionary second edition printed in 1993 and utilized by many libraries, the word race is defined:

"Race. . . 1. a group of persons related by common descent or heredity. 2. a population so related. 3. Anthropol.

a. any of the traditional divisions of humankind, the commonest being the Caucasian, Mongoloid, and Negro, characterized by supposedly distinctive and universal physical characteristics no longer in technical use. b. an arbitrary classification of modern humans, sometimes, esp. formerly, based on any or a combination of various physical characteristics, as skin color, facial form, or eye shape, and now frequently based on such genetic markers as blood groups. c. a human population partially isolated reproductively from other populations, whose members share a greater degree of physical and genetic similarity with one another than with other humans. 4. a group of tribes or peoples forming an ethnic stock: the Slavic race. 5. any people united by common history, language, cultural traits, etc. : the Dutch race. 6. the human race or family; humankind: Nuclear weapons pose a threat to the race. 7. Zool. a variety; subspecies. 8. a natural kind of living creature: the race of fishes. 9. any group, class, or kind: Journalists are an interesting race. 10. the characteristic taste or flavor of wine. —adj. 11. of or pertaining to the races of humankind. [1490 - 1500; < F < It razza, of obscure orig.] — syn. 1. tribe, clan, family. Race, People, Nation are terms for a large body of persons who may be thought of as a unit because of common characteristics. In the traditional biological and anthropological systems of classification Race refers to a group of persons who share such genetically transmitted traits as skin color, hair texture, and eye shape or color; the white race; the yellow race. In reference to classifying the human species, Race is now under dispute among modern biologist and anthropologist. Some feel that the term has no biological validity; others use it to specify only a partially isolated reproductive population whose members share a considerable degree of genetic similarity. In certain broader or less technical senses Race is sometimes used interchangeably with People. People refers to a body of persons united usually by common interests. Ideals, or culture but sometimes also by a common history, language, or ethnic character: We are one people; the peoples of the world; the Swedish people. Nation refers to a body of persons living under an organized government or rule, occupying a defined area, and acting as a unit in matters of peace and war: the English nation." (p.1590)

In reading through this definition one should have ascertained the absence of facts in providing a definitive understanding of the term race. There are no facts to substantiate the use of race as related to humans. The uncertainty in the use of the term is implied by the definition's use of such words as supposedly and arbitrary. While more technical phrases such as physical characteristics (skin color, facial form, or eye shape), genetic markers (in blood groups) and isolation suggest a verification of its usage further inquiry on the use of such technical knowledge suggest such conclusions to be invalid even within the definition itself. It would be inappropriate to assume correctness in the use of such a term as race because of its popularity. Yet this is precisely what has occurred. The meaning and use of the term race has been determined by what folks say.

When searching for a more in-depth view on the term race which would be easily accessible to the average person, one would need to resort to a series of encyclopedias. They represent supposedly an authoritative referenced view. Such meanings are to be viewed as conservative and a preview of general and technical consensus. Here is what several had to say in a brief overview.

The New Caxton Encyclopedia volume 16, 1979.

"race: In biology, a group of geographically defined populations, distinguishable from other such groups by various consistent inherited biological differences, which is actually or potentially capable of interbreeding with other such groups in the species. The demarcation of races on morphological and geographical grounds in any species usually involves some arbitrary distinctions. But the biological species itself is regarded as a fundamental unit of evolution: 'a group of actually or potentially interbreeding natural populations which are reproductively isolated from other such groups.'

The term 'race' is more of a colloquial than a scientific word.

Human groups are not usually described as subspecies as the term is thought (wrongly) to connote a higher level of discontinuity than 'race.' "

Encyclopedia Britannica volume 18, 1973.
"Race: Race as a biological concept in man and other animals refers to the taxonomic (classification) unit immediately below the species. Biologically, a race is a population or a group of populations distinct by virtue of genetic isolation and natural selection: in these terms a race is neither an artificial construct, a collection of individuals arbitrarily selected from a population, nor a religious grouping, linguistic division, or nationality. In man, in which only one species (homo Sapiens) survives, race serves as a major basis for distinguishing one person from another."

Academic American Encyclopedia 1989.
"Race: A race is a population group or subspecies within the living human species, Homo sapiens, set apart from other subspecies on the basis of arbitrarily selected, commonly visible, or phenotypic criteria. The criteria most often selected are skin color, hair quantity and form, and the shape and form of the body, head, and facial features."

Chamber's Encyclopedia New Edition vol. XI (11) 1964.
"Race is a word of uncertain origin. Attempts have been made to associate it, e.g. with the Czech ra'z (stamp, impression), the Arabic ras (head, origin) and the Latin radix (root, foundation) but none of these is acceptable.

Perhaps the most likely suggestion is that it comes from ratio, signifying 'mode;' 'quality;' 'nature;' in which sense it was used by such classical Roman authors as Varro, Cicero and Caesar. Whatever its precise derivation, the form razza is found in 14th - century Italian. By the 15th century it had paved into French and become race. At roughly the same time it occurs as raza in Spanish and race in Portuguese, and in the 16th century the present-day English term was in use.

Zoologically, race is often equated with subspecies, although there is a tendency among some systematists to regard it as a more restricted category for intergrading populations of mammals and fishes. Most anthropologists would agree that all human beings who have lived during the past 10,000 years at least have belonged to a single but polymorphic species, Homo sapiens,. . ."

Clearly our daily used definition on race is based more so in popular meaning lacking in substantive credibility but even more importantly, our usage of the term race in the past as well as in the present suggest that we have a superficial view of ourselves basing who we are on a few (and I emphasize few) phenotypic peculiarity i.e. skin color, facial features, and hair. Even where the term ethnic is used to supplant the term race in an effort to categorize as opposed to isolate, the traits used remain one of superficiality. It is offensive to note that not only is such thinking a product by and large of western civilization but its fallible meaning and use has persisted and been abused in a supposedly scientifically advanced world where we are closer than ever communicatively but ever further adrift in human unity. The concept of Race has effected humankind culturally, educationally, economically, intellectually, socially and religiously.

The idea of race has had its appeal for those seeking to exploit others or seeking to embrace color oriented hatred. A pseudo-scientific definition based primarily on skin color because of misguided popular opinion has persisted despite knowledge to the contrary. It is not simply out of ignorance, although for the masses it may be. For those in positions to sway public opinion, it is out of economic and political gain and greed that such superficial, arbitrary phenotypical traits have come to be perceived as a significant measure of differentiation between human individuals and groups.

The education/scientific arena has been one method by which this idea of race has been perpetuated using a pseudo-scientific or popular definition as its foundation. The intent had been initially to justify one's claim of superiority over others either culturally, religiously, or developmentally both physically and mentally. Physical anthropology while having its merit was in large part developed for such a purpose as to explain the superficial differences as being meaningful and to distinguish one group (their own) above the others based on these differences. Such attempts to read back into history from one's own vantage point has only led to distorted truths and false or pseudo claims. This is why many black-minded individuals refer to history as his-story meaning as told from one's own self interest and not truthfully.

While the idea of race is presently being contradicted by reputable modern studies today, the idea of race still plays an impressionable major role in dividing people on account of these arbitrarily selected superficial traits such as skin color, facial form, hair, etc. Ever since the 14th to 15th century the western civilization had misused the concept of race for exploitive purposes preying upon one's ignorance and quest for simplicity because we have all embraced it. We argue equality even though nothing different can never truly be equal. Like apples and oranges, they are both fruit but they can never be the same as in fully equal. They are different. This fruit analogy would suggest our argument for equality is mute if we insist on sustaining the idea of race. We can never be the same. However humans are meant to be equal being of the same species. We can not be divided into subspecies or any other categories.

It is clear with today's advancing knowledge. Upon preceding into the twenty-first century, we must realize and expose the concept of race as popularly understood and reinforced through a faulty/negligent educational system which has yielded to a popular demand of centuries ago in defining race with the intent of separating people, humans, for self proclaimed purposes.

As ironic as it may appear, this popular definition used by nearly all of us cuts two ways. While one group argues for differences among groups of humans emphasizing the inequality for the sake of feeling superior, the other group reactively embraces the differences too seeking to reconcile their equalness through the effort to substantiate the superiority of a past history. One acting out of hate, despise, and exploitation and the other reactively, defensively but nevertheless still within the boundaries of a definition which has created division although being false from the very beginning. They have both acted and reacted out of ignorance. The understanding in the unity of humans remains a disillusionment because we search for it within a pseudo-scientific term and meaning (race) when being applied to humans.

Yet it has become profitable to act and react to this idea of race. People have been elected or made financial profit through the use of the race card through subtle code words and images if not blatantly in politics, law and order, and indeed in economic planning although pretending business as usual. They even blame those targeted for bringing it up. While some are made to fear differences in people by verbal and visual implications and negative characterizations and references, others are attempting to boaster their differences with positive self imagery. It has become fashionable within the defined Black or African American community to search into one's blackness seeking to reconcile the differences by developing a sense of pride in skin color, facial characteristics or hair type and seeking to establish a romatic history with that African past worthy of recognition. Racism/separation and the seeking of racial equality have both occurred within the framework of a pseudo-scientific term, race, which has been based in the ignorance of supposition and arbitration with no factual basis by which to support grouping humans into distinct categories. Modern studies point out that such efforts are to be considered inappropriate for use in describing individuals and/or groups of humans.

Our society (and world) even now applies imaginative falsehoods and distorted truths within the framework of a pseudo-definition given to us by a society during a time when it searched for a rationale to explain the exploitation of others. In large part although not as insensitive, society today still embraces the term race as is, false or biasly defined back then using skin color to separate. Although we argue for equality, one can not change society's understanding while working within the confines of the present and false concept of race. If we truthfully and sincerely seek equality among all humans, then we must break down the categorizations of humans implied and defined in the concept of race because it has no scientific foundation upon which to exist as a means of describing and/or grouping individuals or humans. It is the intent of this writing that we no longer address ourselves or our relationships in the ignorance shown within the past and present popular views of race.

Chapter Two

Anthropology early on in the development of physical anthropology established the term, race, as a folks definition meaning a view determined by what people in general say. The definition for race was and is a representation of what the society thinks that it is. It is what folks say that it is. "This folk category of the English language refers to discrete groups of human beings who are categorically separated from one another on the basis of arbitrarily selected phenotypic traits. Historically, three 'diagnostic' traits have been used to divide the human species into races: skin color, hair form, and various combinations of nose, face, and lip shapes."[1] The term had no scientific or real measurable value or meaning from the onset and was in large part a reflection of "general sociopolitical biases derived from human social experience and carried over into 'scientific' realms."[2]

Race was a term developed by one group of people to suggest "that some race are inherently superior to others."[3] Herein laid the seeds of racism where one sought based solely on arbitrarily observed physical traits to determine that some people based on race were biologically inferior culturally, religiously, and intellectually. Groups have fought even until today to maintain such thinking in the promotion of states' rights and segregation, ideology of law and order, anti school busing, minorities, capital punishment, and ethnicity. All of this based on what folks say not because it was true or untrue but precipitated by a need to rationalize the institutional enslavement of a people. The impact of this historical occurrence would result in what folks say as the social forces of slavery acted upon them individually and collectively. We would all come to embrace the idea of races viewing individuals or groups as superior or inferior despite strives today towards creating equality. As long as the concept of race exist, we allow for a perpetual argument of one group seemingly being inherently greater or more intelligent than the other.

Regrettably the burden of proof fell upon a scientific community in the past too eager to go along with what folks said in a setting of socio-political biases. Evidence early on in scientific advances and in historical analysis prior to the development of chattel slavery by Europeans stated:

"Research by a number of scholars has shown in detail how institutional circumstances generate racism. One striking example of the rise of racism can be found in the reports of European traders who visited the coast of Africa from the 16th to 19th centuries. The original voyagers were not universally prejudiced against Africans. Indeed many were impressed by the high level of African culture. However when the creation of plantations based on slave labor in the New World transformed the African commodity trade into a traffic in human beings, the attitudes of the Europeans underwent a sharp reversal. It was then that the image of the animal-like African savage became dominant for it allowed the Europeans to rationalize the practice of chattel slavery."[5]

The scientific community through a field of study created to study human diversity called physical anthropology followed the guidelines of an institutional thought in seeking to lend creditable support to this socio-political bias of a developing racism. Claims of inherently biological inferiority was to be established as a society sought to rationalize its dehumanizing actions upon other equals (like humans). Despite one's failure to provide a truthful guideline for racial classifications, the scientific community sought to represent and to legitimate the socio-political biases using as its foundation arbitrary phenotypic characteristics. Even though, "any system of racial classification has a number of built-in weaknesses. All individuals or groups do not neatly fit into definite racial categories. Often the differences between individuals within a race within a population are greater than the average differences between groups defined as races or breeding populations."[5]

A recent case scenario makes an excellent case in point. The December 26 - January 2, 1995 issue of Jet published an article titled: "White Man Who Altered Himself To Look Black Reveals Chilling Account of Racism, Oppresssion."[6] It is an account of a 20 year old white male with obvious white phenotypic characteristics having taken a daily dosage of Psorlen pills to darken his skin color. With a shaven head but with the same style dress, he set out to pretend to be a black man in order to experience first hand the question of discrimination against black males. The Jet quotes him as having said: "It (racism) is considerably worse than I thought it would be. . .He told Jet that he originally intended to do it for a semester, 'but I just couldn't take being constantly pounded with hate. It never seems to stop."[7] He was treated this way simply because of skin color although all the other physical traits i.e. facial features including the nose, lips, head shape typically would not have classified him as having been a black man. He clearly did not fit easily into any one racial classification. Yet science, physical anthropology in particular sought to justify or rationalize an inherent biological inferiority in some individuals or groups of humans using what folks say as their working definition. This unfortunately is the pseudo-scientific explantation which we all still today find ourselves using to determine our existence despite its obvious falsehood and misusages.

Johannes Blumenbach who is described as the father of physical anthropology was supportive of racial classification although such classifications were based on arbitrary traits of human skin color, hair, and shape of one's nose, lips, and/or face. He was clearly a product of his times having failed to rise above societal biases and the need of a society to rationalize and justify its actions from the 16th to 19th century. Physical anthropology was perhaps developed or used as a tool by which to artificially divide humans as groups and/or individuals into static categories. The pretense of research by many such anthropologist contributed greatly towards the belief that certain such groups or individuals were inherently inferior because of one's biological makeup. Such teaching obviously would generate and did generate racist views and ideology. We witness this in the resistance to school bussing which would supposedly mix an inferior group of individuals with those who are said to be superior according to what folks say. States rights which contributed towards segregation laws and once promoted slavery is a racist concept which today is still an overflow from the term (race) grounded in arbitrary and supposed common physical traits. The prejudices of individuals and the social forces which generate systematic and institutionalize oppression are all based in the pseudo-scientific term, race, which as cited earlier in the example given can not be stated as being pure and/or static.

While one could state perhaps justifiably so that science had not advanced sufficiently to understand the mistakes and errors in its attempts to subdivide humans into static groups during the time frame (16th to 19th century) in which the definition for race evolved, it must be pointed out that "genes, the units of heredity, are transmitted from parents to offspring"[8] was discovered as early as 1865 by Gregory Mendel. This led to the development of research in population genetics beginning "in 1908 with the formulation of the Hardy-Weinberg law for predicting the frequencies of genes and of their combinations in individuals genotypes within populations."[9] A plausible answer to the human variability was made available early on and physical anthropology was made aware of its potential usage by the 1950s. Yet the pseudo-scientific definition persisted and still does today as people are being divided into groups according to an arbitrary selection of what is at most meaningless and superficial physical traits.

In the 1930s many cultural anthropologist sought "to explain human variation in natural scientific, notably racial and, hence, biological terms."[10] While the primary interest for them was the study of culture, one finds concealed in the thinking an attempt to describe humans which appear different as other cloaking it with the ethnocentric disguise of culture but nevertheless seeking to categorize individuals into static groupings. Yet just as there can be no pure race neither can there be any one culture to have existed purely nor to have existed as a monolith, static. A J.S. Kahn points to a resurgence in the use of culture as a tool to divide individuals into groupings again in the 1960s and 1970s. Of course it is during this period of time that those ethnically identified as African-Americans or Blacks sought to gain a political identity under the concept of multiculturalism. We wanted representation in historical studies, academic institutions, social awareness, and political representation as a separate and identifiable culture within this scheme of mulitculturalism. Unfortunately in our blind rush for equal status in this society as a newly self discovered black people, we were playing right into the hands of those seeking to explain human variation in biological terms and thereby separate those who differ into groups identified as others . This way of thinking "is fraught with dangers both theoretical and practical. It risks essentializing the idea of culture as the property of an ethnic group or race. . ."[11] By allowing and even aiding one in considering you as the other, puts one in a position not only to be labeled as different in biological terms and infe-

33

rior but also in a position to be excluded as the other. One can never be considered an equal as the other because you will always be defined as being inherently inferior in one way or another by those seeking to view themselves as being superior. It is liken to two basketball players, one black and one white showing great ability in the sport. The white player is said to be exercising great skill and intelligence while the black player is believed to be exercising raw talent or innate skills. The message being that raw, innate skills are more animal-like being instinctive and therefore inferior to the skills of the white player even though the black player may be the smarter player of the two. The point being that there are risks involved in the embracing of an understanding in which one is determined to be the other especially when being viewed from the perspective of a pseudo-scientific term, race, which is the underlying theme when speaking about ethnicity and/or culture. Each seeks to statically categorize or classify individuals into groups. We will see that race is a false understanding and explanation for human variation. Yet we are caught up in the fantasy world of those seeking to interpret the historical abuse of chattel slavery on the basis of phenotypic characteristics such as skin color. Having been misguided, we believe those differences are real and substantial. We have in our ignorance complied with such thinking seeking to prove and show our own favorable distinctiveness although a scientific understanding points to a view which is contrary to our present and past socio-political beliefs.

Chapter Three

When conducting a survey of physical anthropology, it can be suggested that while not becoming a recognized science until the eighteenth century. Its impetus can be linked with the development of scientific study in the western world. Scientific focus on human development had not been a concern before this. Human study before was more of a theological concern. Clearly ancient travel early on would result in an awareness of phenotype differences but initial theological reflection concluded one human creation despite the observable differences. This would remain the dominant thought until western scientific advances began to question the differences on the basis of natural order. Such studies were initiated from the context of attempting to understand themselves by studying or the observing of others. Subsequently by the twelfth century, the first attempt was made at dividing people scientifically.

A Gillaume de Couches[1] in the twelfth century used the term polygenesis to describe these observable differences in human physical characteristics. This marked perhaps the first noted attempt to consciously suggest dividing people into separate groups based upon observable phenotype variations. Polygenesis as the term suggested over against mongenesis implied an orientation towards a multiple geographical origin and development for humans as opposed to one common origin and/or development in which we have the same modern ancestral heritage. "This position is maintained, with little elaboration by Paracelsus and Giordane Bruno in the sixteenth century. Polygenesis finally became a popular theory as a result of Isaac de La Peyrere's exposition published in 1655."[2] One of the earliest attempts to classify people into racially distinctive groupings was performed by a Fracois Bernier who further embellished on the theory of polygenesis in the year 1684. "He divided mankind into Europeans, Africans, Asiatics, and Lapps. His taxonomy laid the groundwork for the eighteenth-century classifications by the naturalists Linnaeus and Blumenbach, which are the basis of modern racial classification."[3]

It was Johann Friedrich Blumenbach,[4] a German anthropologist, who formulated a color category to describe the polygenetic human grouping. He used the colors black, brown, red, yellow and white. This was the beginning of classifying humans according to the arbitrary phenotype of skin color. Natural history as regards the taxonomy of the human was the lynch-pin theory which would propel the concept of race into the nineteenth century. Phenotypic variations were now being described and defined as biological differences as in speciation. This set the stage for systematic and institutionalized racism. One's culture and social status even the ability to learn was being correlated with these phenotype differences believed now to be biological. All during the period of chattel slavery the whispers of superior/inferior as relates to the classification of these human groups was becoming louder. Now it was being justified by rational thought grounded in natural history.

An interesting hindsight view of the past period in which the development of racial thoughts were initiated is that the mind set or intent would not have been one of racism or racist ideology but rather an outcome of ignorance which prevailed in the effort to elevated one's self above others. During this particular time period they believed they were not only correct but they believed they were being truthful in their explanation of the differences. This was understood to be the natural order of things. Race was viewed from primitive to modern humans with the so-called white race being the modern human. It was the order of the day still believed by many and was accepted by the world. Things have not changed even in the twentieth and going into the twenty-first century. "Typologies and hierarchies of race were presented as self-evidently appropriate at the beginning of the century, and cultural analysis along racial lines conveyed no particular stigma. . . Race was perceived to be a biological category, a natural phenomenon unaffected by social forces."[5] Herein lies perhaps the real irony because it was in large part the social forces which pressed the scientific world of the Europeans into action to explain racial differences not because it was true but because they needed a rationale to justify a belief in their superior status. Even though there were grumblings by a physical anthropologist and social activist named Franz Boas who believed in the equality of the races although believing slavery and prejudicial laws and practice had impeded the mental growth of the so-called black race, the notion of superior/inferior in terms of a hierarchal structure as regards the categorization of people into races carried the day becoming the teaching of the everyday and ordinary citizen even to this day. We believe that there is a difference in the races physically and mentally.

In fact from the beginning until very recent times physical anthropology which today is often referred to as human biology would have best been described as racial anthropology or racial biology then would today be described as scientific racism. It was more a reflection of the social forces to separate humans than a scientific investigation examining the facts. An understanding or belief in the superior/inferior of the races was demonstrated in the teachings of an anthropologist in 1943 named Fay-Cooper Cole[6] who espoused that the white race was the primary branch from which all other races are derived. Scientific racism was not only taught in the classroom regardless of its offensive nature being untrue and grounded in arbitrary selection. During World War II under the rules of segregation, it was being practiced by the medical corps. "The medical corps kept separate blood supplies for black and white troops."[7] The idea of polygenesis and races based in the belief of biological differences was developing and would be sustained by the social forces of a developing institutional racism.

An anthropologist named Ruth Benedict discussed a segregated military with information contained in a pamphlet she published during World War II. She sought to discount the supposed wide gulf between the so-called races which promoted an ideology of superior/inferior based on biological differences and the purity of the races. Yet the social forces of institutional racism would prevent the distribution of the pamphlet to a segregated military. Such considerations were deemed inappropriate in a society which allowed the teachings of scientific racism based in arbitrary phenotypes made to seem as a biologically significant difference.

The concept of race is a rationalization attempting to justify the beliefs and practices of a society both in the past and in the present because the racist thoughts and actions which are ongoing result from the ignorance of self indulgence in seeking to differentiate humans. In fact the fervor of such institutional and individual thinking in the concept of race was directly responsible for the known holocaust committed by the Nazi Germans in World War II (not to mention the forgotten holocaust of the African slave trade). Yet scientific racism was not embraced in the nineteenth century by the Nazi Germans only but was evident "in France, England, Japan and the United States."[8] However the castastrophe of world wide racism was made overtly evident in the events of Nazi Germany to the world through graphic pictorial presentations.

Although greater atrocities in terms of sheer numbers if not in the horrid acts occurred during the African salve trade and middle passage, race was no longer simply taken for granted. In fact the definition and studies on race began being called into question as representing a pseudo-scientific terminology.

This "led to an international effort to ground biocultural research on racial variation in more adequate scientific theory and a more human ethic. UNESCO formed a committee of social scientists for this purpose in 1949. Ashley Montagu, an American Anthropologist, wrote the first position paper made public in 1950. Then the second committee was formed of biologists and anthropologists who worked with Ashley Montagu to revise the statement on race, and circulate it among other scientists for peer review so that a final version could be released in 1951. This effort to reach a scientific consensus that would turn away from the social ideology, garbled biology and typological thinking that had proven to be so disastreous, emphasized that the real units of human evolution are not racial types but local interbreeding populations. Variation within these populations is the key fact to be studied, not typological uniformity, since variation provides the stuff that allows processes of natu ral selection to operate."[9]

We had witnessed from a recent historical perspective the use of race, understood to be a pseudo-scientific term, as a rationale for the genocide of a people. Certainly the world would not wish to consciously nor unconsciously fall prey to such social forces being led astray again. Yet despite the effort of UNESCO to rid the world of this pseudo-scientific term, race, almost a half century ago, it still remains as entrenched as a dormant virus or bacterial resistant to all efforts to stamp it out. Unfortunately the UNESCO findings are not binding on states' internal affairs.

As recent as 1985 a book titled *Anthropological Glossary* written by a Roger Pearson, Ph.D. for The Institute for the Study of Man in Washington, D.C. was intended to provide one with definitions used in the field of anthropology. His definition for race was as follows:

"Race, a genetically distinct inbreeding division within a species. The term 'race' is often used interchangeably with 'subspecies.' Successive hominid races have arisen throughout the course of hominid evolution due to anagenesis, or phyletic evolution (taking place in different directions and at different rates within different populations), and kladogenesis, or 'branching,' due to geographical or even cultural isolation. While many animal subspecies may be regarded as recipient species, hominid behavior has been modified by cultural accretions, some of which (e.g. 'race prejudice') have served to facilitate speciation while others, such as those which have reduced the significance of geographical barriers, have tended to reduce genetic isolation, by enabling more successful subspecies to expand into other territories, where they have customarily mixed their genes with those of the autochthonous populations. The living hominids have been conceptually classified into various major geographical races, such as Astraloids, Caucasoids, Mongoloids, Negroids and Negritoids, subdivided into innumerable local races. These in turn tend to be made up of clusters of microraces, which are closer to the genetic reality of Mendelian or near-Mendelian populations, and are the essential basis of all race differences."[10]

This is without question a large step backwards not only from the determination made by the scientific discovery of UNESCO following World War II but it further suggest evidence of racism on a conscious level when in 1976 the definition made available for use by anthropologist according to the Encyclopedia of Anthropology states:

"Race. This folk category of the English language refers to discrete groups of human beings who are categorically separated from one another on the basis of arbitrarily selected phyenotypic traits. Historically, three 'diagnostic' traits have been used to divide the human species into races: skin color, hair form and various combinations of nose, face and lip shapes.

Increasingly, physical anthropologists and biologists are reassessing the concept of race and finding it of no scientific use whatever. There are both empirical and theoretical reasons for this rejection of the concept. Empirically as research on population genotypes accumulates, it is becoming increasingly clear that the growing number of known gene frequencies do not cluster together into polar groupings: although any two or three specific genes might have high correlations of cooccurence, other gene distributions will fall into widely varying patterns. Thuse as we learn more and more about human gene distributions, it becomes less and less possible to divide the species into discrete, genetically defined groups (races),

On the theoretical level the concept of race raises problems because it treats as 'explained' questions that are not. Moreover it causes us to neglect problems that need solving and also obfuscates the distinction between genotype and phenotype. Finally, it treats as static ('pure races') the biological aspects human groups which evolutionary theory tells us must be viewed dynamically. Even when applied by 'experts,' the notion of race results in wildly differing categorizations of the 'races of the human species.' "[11]

Even in 1972 it was stated by R.C. Lewontin who was on an Evolutionary Biology committee at the University of Chicago in Chicago, Illinois: "Human racial classification is of no social value and is positively destructive of social and human relations. Since such racial classification is now seen to be of virtually no genetic or taxonomic significance either, no justification can be offered for its continuance."[12]

While the concept of race is perhaps the result of what folks say meaning people in general, one should still be able to conclude that the concept of race in light of advanced understandings should no longer exist as a term used in reference to a group of people. Efforts to categorize people into specific classifications are known to be invalid and untruthful. However as the definition of 1986 indicates, the concept of race and the usage of racial classification lives on. This is the result of institutional racism and the pressures of social forces upon the individual. When one lives in a racist society one tends to learn prejudicial behavior. Our academic institutions still espouse race despite it being a pseudo-scientific term; the media still feeds on racial distinctions although such characteristics are arbitrarily selected; the church has historically engaged in separation on account of skin color even attempting to make up portraits of Jesus which reflect one's own phenotypic characteristics; and even the job market unfairly and all too often has disqualified someone on the basis of skin color. We have a system, a social force in place, which drives the concept of race for selfish purposes. It is institutional racism which keeps the pseudo-scientific term, race, thriving and facilitates what folks say about others' differences. Clearly most people in general simply do not know any better having gotten caught up in the system both black and white. We simply go along with the system for the most part fulfilling the roles which folks say we should as racial types. Although the scientific community knows better because the research is clear, like general folk they too have been influenced by the social forces of racism developing theories which seek to declare social inequality and the lesser intelligence of some on the basis of race. It is our beliefs and not our knowledge which has not changed. They want to believe based upon the phenotypic traits that a biological difference exist although the facts are to the contrary. People have been oppressed by law because of such ignorance and false inventions having been embraced.

Our mind-set appears to be the by-product of this institutional racism which got its genesis from a developing western ideology in its attempts to classify people according to phenotype characteristics and to define themselves by looking to the immediate past only. An institution ran by socio-economic and political influences had continued defining people according to race and racial characteristic despite scientific advances in research discounting and disapproving of the use of race. Nevertheless there are still those who will not yield to such truth. "Thinly disguised racism still nibbles at the crumbs of respectable science in ways which retain the language of race in academic, political and public discourse."[13]

This institutional racism fuels individuals' prejudices allowing one to think and act upon prejudments favorable or unfavorable towards another individual or group of seemingly like individuals. Where the arbitrary phenotypic selections suggest an individual or group of individuals to be of a different racial category, an unfavorable prejudment will in most instances be the case. Such categorical responses are being institutionally prescribed setting the stage for how we view and act towards one another where such phenotype characteristics are noted. It does not occur when one is assumed to be of the same category. A case in point being where an individual identified as an African American passes for white because one's appearance places him in this category. He does not experience the social forces of institutional racism until his identity is made known in a separate location suggesting that racism is systematic.

The social forces of institutional racism is given credence in G.W. Allport's The Nature of Prejudice discussion on "The Process of Categorization."[14] We tend to categorize things for prejudging to avoid the necessity of having to make an analysis of every bit of new information or experience encountered. Such categories are products of the society at large. To keep it simple, we cluster these categories adding new thought to them only by modifying the old ones. We tend to generalize with these categories as to cover the broadest territory possible such as with race coloring these generalizations with feelings charged with emotions. While much of our thinking may even be rational, we fail to separate the rational thought from the irrational. The point being made here is that the tendency to categorize is in large part influenced by the social forces of the society at large which is being relegated by institutional practices, teachings, and definitions. Lest we forget the historical tragedies brought to fruition because of the social forces of institutional racism in the slave trade and in Nazi Germany, such thinking and practices are bound to mount a destructive campaign on human lives again and again. Just as black skin was made to seem as a racial divide so was being a Jew both having been invented.

It must be made clear! "The latest information available supports the traditional findings of anthropologists and other social scientist - that there is no scientific basis of any kind for racial discrimination. . . The evolution of races is due, according to modern genetics, to mutation, selection, migration, and genetic drift. It is easy to shift from this statement of genetic theory to complications of hemoglobin, blood groups or other technical information. . . Genetics shows us that typology must be completely removed from our thinking if we are to progress."[15]

One thing is certain from this historical survey of anthropology specifically physical anthropology. Our history in the western world establishment has led to the development of institutional racism and has allowed our present to be congruent with our past. We have established a foundation rooted in a concept which we now knowingly reject definitionally and scientifically. Yet it and its dangers persist because we are comfortable with it! To simply categorize people in groups is to make it easier to identify, like or dislike them on the basis of prejudgmental characteristics.

We should understand that this categorization results in new thoughts being absorbed by simply modifying old ones rather than new thoughts replacing and ruling out the old ones as being invalid and inappropriate for use in the more knowledgeable and scientifically advanced society. Instead we see prejudices once based on skin color becoming racial type, from racial type to ethnic/cultural classification or majority versus minority, all along down through history being based in the original concept of race suggesting a biological difference creating a superior/inferior division or ranking. The words colored, Black, African American, white, European, ethnicity, culture, conservative, fundamental, or minority/majority allow for the same antiquated prejudices and racial discrimination being simply stated in modified terms. These are new terms modifying old thoughts but nevertheless based on the same old principle to divide because of phenotypic differences. We can conclude that such terms as stated above, being modifications on the central theme race, are pseudo-scientific as well and ought not to exist in a knowledgeable and advanced society. New thoughts must not modify old ones but replace and obliterate old ones found to be archaic as is the concept of race. We can not rid ourselves of institutional racism until we rid of that which feeds it, our history living in the present. Human relationships are not to be simplified and as such can never be divided and categorized. We are not the same but we are individuals of the same.

Chapter Four

With the supposed advancements of the so-called Black race or African American and minorities in the job market, academically, economically, and up the corporate ladder, one might conclude that all this talk about race and racism is simply a lot of bunk. Such people may even go so far as to suggest that this society as a whole has become interracially tolerate. Affirmative action, set asides and equal opportunity are even being debated as reverse discrimination in view of such advancements. However the sustaining presence of race and the concept thereof remains intact and vibrant. While some according to a recent study by V. Bakanic[1] stated that racism is alive and well today in the desire of segregated schools and residential areas. Not all respondents to a survey given were equally adamant in their views on segregation but the shades of gray show evidence of racism only now on a sliding scale of tolerate to intolerate. Nevertheless racism has never been abated or excised only subdued because favorable circumstances which existed for a period following the surges of civil rights movements which require renewing throughout history.

The idea of race having become institutionally integrated into a society has become socially acceptable surfacing as a concern primarily when faced with increasing levels of problems i.e. unemployment or justice facilitating increase levels of intolerance. Otherwise racism remains according to V. Bakanic a socially acceptable attitude as long as one remains towards the tolerate end of the scale on race. "It has been argued that the gap between tolerant attitudes and persistent discrimination is merely a parroting of socially acceptable attitudes. One popular argument even asserts that our education system has caused people to censure their attitudes or at the very least silence attitudes that are not 'politically correct' (D'Souza, 1991)."[2] Racism is simply being disguised or dressed up as to become more acceptable but allowing a society to in fact remain racist below the surface.

It is important at this point to define and/or determine who can and can not be defined as a racist because the term racist today is being expanded to become inclusive of those who have been merely reactionaries in their quest for equality within the context of a description put upon them. It should be clear that racism is absolutely prevalent in this society and even the world having an effect upon everyone having become institutionalized but not everyone or every group being identified as a race can be described as a racist individual or group. A racist is to be understood as anyone or group who subscribes to being a member of a so-called race which believes itself to be superior on the basis of biological differences to all other so-called races. Those who find themselves the subject of this tolerance or acceptance because it is politically correct can not be a racist but a reactionist. Racism has its origin in western ideology, an ideology advocating superiority in physical and mental development and culture not to mention industry and technology. Those who believe themselves to be the standard bearers of western world development are likewise to be understood as the standard bearers of racist ideology directly or indirectly.

48

This is a point of great concern for the world if not specifically this society at large because what happens when acceptance is no longer politically correct and the concept of race although false and invalid continues to exist and be applied discriminately on the basis of phenotypic characteristics. As we examine history, we will find that such a concern is indeed warranted.

Keeping in mind that the concept of race was under suspicion earlier on in its initial development, we have experienced many ebbs in our attempts to move humanity forward towards an understanding of its blackness. The following is an example of our inability to progress despite the appearance that we might be on our way:

"Thomas Jefferson's attitudes to blacks varied during his lifetime. In his early years, Jefferson thought blacks were biologically inferior, then decided that slavery had a destructive conditioning effect which stamped blacks with 'odious peculiarities.' With this view, and spurred by his conviction that 'natural rights' accrued to all men, Jefferson penned a short, passionate attack on King George III's indulgence of the slave traffic, for inclusion in the Declaration of Independence. But, at the behest of delegates from South Carolina and Georgia, and with the indulgence of northern delegates whose ports sheltered and profited from slave ships, the clause was omitted from the final version."

It read;

"He (King George III) has waged cruel war against human nature itself, violating its most sacred rights of life and liberty in the persons of a distant people who never offended him, captivating and carrying them into slavery in another hemisphere, or to incur miserable death in their transportation thither. This piratical warfare, the opprobrium of infidel powers, is the warfare of the Christian king of Great Britain. Determined to keep open a market where MEN should be bought and sold, he has prostituted his negative suppressing every legislative attempt to prohibit or restrain this execrable commerce."[3]

"1865, Washington, D.C. Death of Abraham Lincoln. The New President Andrew Johnson, calls for ratification of the Thirteenth Amendment, which forbids slavery, but opposes black suffrage."[4]

"1866, Washington, D.C. Passage of the Civil Rights Bill of 1866 despite President Johnson's veto. Its intention is to nullify the black codes. A bill is introduced in the District of Columbia to provide for black suffrage. White voters are asked to indicate their sentiments in a referendum. Over 6,500 vote against extension of the franchise to blacks; only 35 favor it. The fourteenth Amendment passes the House and Senate despite opposition from Johnson. After considerable wrangling, a compromise bill, modestly extending the authority of the Freedmen's Bureau, is passed over a Johnson veto. The bill provides for military protection of blacks, distribution of food to members of both races, expansion of educational facilities, and return of expropriated land to original owners."[5]

It should be noted that the Freedmen's Bureau was recognized as the first "federal civil rights agency for blacks. Congress created the bureau in March 1865 under its official title, the Bureau of Refugees, Freedmen, and Abandoned Lands. It initially fed, clothes, sheltered, and gave medical to more whites than blacks, it became identified only with freedmen after Congress directed it to promote their general welfare. . . Many of the oldest historically black colleges and universities owe a debt to the bureau. A feeble congressional and national commitment to full and equal citizenship for blacks permitted the bureau to die after 1868."[6]

"BLACK CODES. During 1865 and 1866, all southern states except North Carolina passed a number of laws designed as substitutes for the old slave codes. The main purpose of these so-called Black Codes was to ensure an immobile, dependent black labor force for each state's agricultural interest. They were designed to immobilize penniless, unemployed, and powerless black laborers. If charged with being vagrants, such individuals had to post a bond or offer the required security. . . While most Black Codes made no distinction based on race, they were worded in such a way as to exempt white workers."[7]

"1867, Washington, D.C. Congress passes, over another veto by President Johnson, the first Reconstruction Act, which provides for military rule pending organization of state governments loyal to the Union. The Act requires occupied states to ratify the Fourteenth Amendment and guarantee the vote of blacks. Secretary of War Sumner fails on efforts to have Act order Freedman's Bureau to provide homes and schools for blacks."[8]

"1867, Southern and Border states. Enforcement of the Reconstruction Act provides Blacks with majority of vote in most southern states and alliances of black and white Republicans control in border states."[9]

"1868, Southern States, Oscar Dunn, an ex-slave and captain in the Union army, is elected Lieutenant Governor of Louisiana. Blacks out number whites 81 to 40 in South Carolina Legislature, but whites have majority in state senate."[10]

"1868, Washington, D.C. The Fourteenth Amendment is ratified, establishing the concept of 'equal protection' for all citizens under the U.S. Constitution. President Johnson's veto of the bill granting vote to blacks in the District of Columbia is overridden by Congress. Congress passes the Fifteenth Amendment guaranteeing the vote to blacks and a bill denying the Supreme Court the right to rule on cases involving constitutionality of the Reconstruction Act."[11]

"1870, Washington, D.C. The Fifteenth Amendment, guaranteeing all citizens the right to vote is ratified. In 'Ku Klux Klan Acts, the Army is empowered to maintain order in federal elections. The Supreme Court refuses to review the Reconstruction Acts. . . Between 1870 and 1900, 22 blacks, 13 of them ex-slaves, are to serve in Congress. The Census of 1870 finds only 19% of blacks literate. The figure reaches 43% in 1890."[12]

"1872, Washington, D.C. Congress passes Amnesty Act, enabling officials of the Confederacy to hold office. Ku Klux Klan Act expires and is not renewed."[13]

"1874, Virginia State rearranges election districts and local government system thereby reducing political power of blacks."[14]

"1875, Washington, D.C. Congress passes the Civil Rights Bill of 1875, prohibiting discrimination in such public accommodations as hotels, theaters, and amusement parks. A key piece of legislation in the post-Civil War era, it seeks to '. . .mete out equal and exact justice to all, of whatever nativity, race, color, or persuasions, religious or political. . ."[15]

"1876, Washington, D.C. The Senate, after three years of controversy, refuses to seat H.R. Pinchback, a black who had been elected in Louisiana in 1873. In two decisions, the Supreme Court decides that the Fourteenth and Fifteenth Amendments do not guarantee suffrage. In U.S. vs. Cruikshank the Court declares that the Fourteenth Amendment provides blacks with equal protection under the law but does not add anything 'to the rights which one citizen has under the Constitution against another.' The Court rules that 'the right of suffrage is not a necessary attribute of national citizenship."[16]

"1877, The United States. Many historians regard 1877 as the start of a prolonged, adverse period, in which the legal and economic status of blacks declines. Major factors involved are the re-establishment of white political control in the South and the widespread use of blacks as cheap labor and strike breakers in the nation's rapid economic expansion."[17]

"1877, Washington, D.C. In the aftermath of the inconclusive presidential election of 1876, Rutherford Hayes, a Republican, promises southern delegates he will withdraw federal troops from the South. This contributes to .his selection for the presidency over Samuel J. Tilden by the House of Representatives. Democrats control Congress, deny funds to the Army, and in 1878 remove presidential authority to use troops to guarantee fair elections."[18]

"1878, Washington, D.C. The U.S. Attorney General reveals widespread intimidation of blacks attempting to vote and stuffing of ballot boxes in several southern states."[19]

"1881, Washington, D.C. Chester Arthur succeeds Garfield, who is assassinated and implies the belief that blacks are not sufficiently educated to vote."[20]

"1883, Washington, D.C. The Supreme Court declares the Civil Rights Act of 1875 unconstitutional."[21]

"1884, Washington, D.C. Former black Reconstruction Congressman John Roy Lynch is elected temporary chairman of the Republican convention—the first black to preside over a national political gathering."[22]

"1890, Washington, D.C. In the In Re Green decision, the Supreme Court sanctions control of elections by state officials, thus weakening federal protection for southern black voters. The Court also permits states to segregate public transportation facilities."[23]

"1891, Washington, D.C. The number of lynchings in the United States is reported to be 112. The great majority of victims are blacks residing in the south."[24]

"1894, Washington, D.C. A section of the Emancipation Act dealing with the right of blacks to vote is repealed."[25]

"1896, Washington, D.C. The Supreme Court in the *Plessy v Ferguson* decision upholds the doctrine of 'separate but equal.' paving the way for segregation of blacks in all walks of life. Justice Harlan dissenting, calls the ruling as 'pernicious as the Dred Scott case."[26]

"1901, Washington, D.C. Congressman George White delivers his farewell address in the House of Represen tatives. . . No black was to serve in Congress again until 1928."[27]

"1907, Washington, D.C. The Supreme Court upholds the right of railroads to segregate passengers traveling between states even when this runs counter to the laws of states in which the train is traveling."[28]

"1909, The United States Sambo and Rastus comedy starts, in which blacks are depicted as childlike and incompetent, became popular."[29]

"1919, The United States Membership of the NAACP approaches 100,000 despite attempts in some areas, such as Texas, to make it illegal. During the second half of the year, there are 75 lynchings and 27 race riots, the severest in Chicago and Washington, D.C. Charles Evans Hughes, leading jurist and defeated Presidential candidate, supports the NAACP efforts to have lynching outlawed."[30]

"1922, Washington, D.C. After it is approved by the House, Republican Senators vote to abandon the Dyer Anti-Lynching Bill, which provides severe penalties and fines for 'any state or municipal officer' convicted of negligence in affording protection to individuals in custody who are attacked by a mob bent on lynching, torture, or physical intimidation. The Bill had also provided for compensation to the families of victims."[31]

"1924, Washington, D.C. Immigration Act excludes blacks of African descent from entering the country."[32]

"1926, Washington, D.C. President Coolidge tells Congress that the country must provide 'for the amelioration of race prejudice and the extension to all elements of equal opportunity and equal protection under the laws, which are guaranteed by the Constitution.' Twenty-three blacks are reported lynched during this year."[33]

"1942, Chicago Founding of the Congress of Racial Equality (CORE), a civil rights group dedicated to a direct-action, nonviolent program. In 1943, CORE stages its first sit-in in a Chicago restaurant."[34]

"1944, Washington, D.C. Restrictions of black seamen to shore duty are ended, as is exclusion of blacks from the Coast Guard and Marine Corps. The War Department officially ends segregation in all Army posts, but the order is widely ignored. The U.S. Supreme Court rules that 'white primaries' violate the Fifteenth Amendment."[35]

"1954, Washington, D.C. On May 17, by a unanimous 9 to 0 vote, the Supreme Court declares that 'separate but equal' educational facilities are 'inherently unequal' and that segregation is therefore unconstitutional. The decision is reached in the case of Brown v. Board of Education, (of Topeka) and overturns the 'separate but equal' doctrine that since 1896 has legitimized segregation. In another case, the court rules that the University of Florida must admit blacks regardless of any 'pubic mischief' it might cause."[36]

"1954, Washington, D.C. . . .The Department of Defense reports that 'all-Negro' units in the Army no longer exist. However, some bases still evade integration. The Veteran's Administration announces their hospitals have been desegregated, but the Department of Health, Education and Welfare declares it will continue to give funds to segregated hospitals. . ."[37]

"1955, Washington, D.C. U.S. Supreme Court orders school boards to draw up desegregation procedures 'with all deliberate speed.' In accordance with Supreme Court edicts, the Interstate Commerce Commission outlaws segregated buses and waiting rooms for interstate passengers, but many communities ignore the order."[38]

"1955, Washington, D.C. The Eisenhower administration continues to discourage civil rights legislation. The House of Representatives defeats attempts by Adam Clayton Powell, Jr. to deny funds to segregated schools."[39]

"1956, Washington, D.C. U.S. Supreme Court rules bus segregation unconstitutional. Montgomery boycott ends in victory for boycotters on December 21."[40]

"1957, Washington, D.C. A civil rights bill, affirming the rights to vote, is enacted after provisions strengthening school integration are withdrawn."[41]

"1958, Southern States. Black voters registration rises slowly, as states institute complicated delaying tactics. Black registration reaches 72% in Tennessee, 39% in Florida and 36% in North Carolina and Texas, but is only 3% in Mississippi."[42]

"1959, Southern States. Blacks are elected to local offices in North Carolina. In other areas, however, blacks are disenfranchised and in Tennessee, black landowners registering to vote are denied their usual preharvest loans. In Virginia, Prince Edward County abolishes its public school system rather than comply with an integration order."[43]

"1960, Washington, D.C. President Eisenhower signs a bill authorizing judges to appoint referees to aid blacks to register and vote in federal elections. The bill also outlaws bombing and mob action to restrict voting."[44]

"1963, Birmingham, Alabama. Four black children are killed in the bombing of the 16th street Baptist Church."[45]

"1964, Washington, D.C. A major Civil Rights Bill, forbidding discrimination in public accommodations and employment, is enacted with strong support from President Johnson, as the Senate finally votes cloture to shut off filibuster by southern opponents."[46]

The basis of this, I give it and I take it away, turn of events as indicated above is the concept of race institutionalized and socialized. When it is politically acceptable, gains are made in an attempt to disregard phenotypic differences but when the level of racism increases previous gains are then either challenged, modified or out right reversed calling upon even stronger legislation the next time as in the instances of civil rights laws, voting rights laws, or school desegregation laws. When the guarantee of one's rights must be frequently renewed having been denied initially because of skin color basically then the issue of race remains a barrier.

Using D.E. Muir[47] description of racism, we should understand these ebbs on the basis of mean racists verses kind racists. The ebbs in our history occur when the agenda of the mean racists prevail resulting in efforts to delete, erase, or question human gains to put all humans on one accord for opportunity. Yet it must be made clear again that all who subscribe to being members of a so-called race which professes to be biologically superior are racist to a degree. They are somewhere on the sliding scale between the mean racist and the kind racist. I use sliding scale to suggest even the kind racist can rapidly become the mean racist when territory which they deemed their's is intruded upon by one of another race considered to be inferior. For example: a long awaited promotion is denied because of past injustices in a company and the promotion is given instead to a so-called minority of color; or a person of color is accused of killing a loved one who is of the so-called opposite race. Such instances can cause kind racists to slide from kind to mean. This hatred is without reasoning and is based simply on so-called racial traits. As long as a society or the world harbors the belief in the concept of race using it to divide and categorize humans, racism will continue to exist from tolerate to intolerate.

Hence depending upon the political climate racism can slide either way on the scale or cause the kind racist to simply turn a deaf ear allowing racism not only to be perpetuated but at times to be blatant and obvious in one's actions and words uncensored. Meanwhile the mean racists, also out of ignorance to the invalidity of the term race, is ever vigilant often times behind the scene mounting campaigns for the separation of humans on the basis of color seeking to thwart or dismantle progress made by those attempting to level the playing field in education, employment, justice and ownership. They instigate fear to create false apprehension and at times even plot the destruction of another so-called race's leader by character assassination, entrapment, etc. to weaken any efforts and campaigns a people of color might endeavor to bring about a parity among all people regardless of variations in phenotype traits.

Nevertheless the equation of race will forever stimulate notions of inequality even though it has been falsely injected and institutionalized by the very means by which we govern ourselves as a society and develop our methods and formulas for relating to one another (state and federal laws and education). The concept of race must go the way of slavery and apartheid to be dismantled along with all related language. It is my hope that the discussion presented here will kindle our interest to engage in such a process for the sake of humanity.

Up until now, no one, black or white has sought to defuse the inflammatory, emotionally charged and separatist language which has developed in large part because of the concept of race by openly attacking race as an invalid concept and calling for a national discussion at all levels to erase it from our imagery, definitions, and way of thinking. While scientists, governmental agencies i.e. the census bureau and elements of the academic world have known, none have put forth the needed effort to dismantle the institutionalized racism caused by the term, race. Instead we seek to use more subtle terms i.e. ethnic, culture, minority, etc. It is perhaps now through reading this writing that the general public and various students will finally become cognant of the fact that we have been hoodwinking ourselves over these past centuries by ignorantly believing in the fallacious term, race, and in large part structuring our world around this concept. We need to consider what science already knows and why science in general has for the most part ceased to use the term race knowing there is no biological difference by which to categorically divide people. There are only insignificant variations in phenotype being made to seem real by an uninformed society. Such findings are an indictment of our society and indeed the world for having allowed ourselves to be misguided.

Chapter Five

"A variety of data (genetic markers, nuclear DNA, and mitochondrial DNA) all suggest low levels of population differentiation in modern humans, often less than found among subspecies of other organisms. . . These findings have had several implications, for the study of human variation and human evolution. First such low levels of population differentiation imply that the vast majority of genetic variation is among individuals within groups and not due to variation among groups. As such, these findings show little support for the concept of race or racial classifications. . ."[1] Secondly it should be noted that genetic markers include blood groups. The differences in Humans are not distinct characteristics which account for biological separation allowing for classification by group. Instead they are merely variations of the same. Humans are to be understood as having multiple sizes, shapes and colors, multiple phenotype characteristics which are simply a montage of human variation. These variations have no qualitative value allowing for distinctiveness by which one can classify or categorize humans into groups and thereby define who they are.

The concept of race is a nonsensical word. The operative phrase for understanding human phenotype is human variation. (It will be explained later that not all human variations are the result of random and/or natural selective mutational changes). Hence the human is a montage of colors, sizes, shapes and physical characteristics but yet is only to be understood as one species and not subspecies under the umbrella of species. We must not let appearances deceive us into believing in racial classifications or distinct differences.

In fact when giving consideration to human variation as a point in fact, one will realize how migration studies demonstrate how such variations in physical characteristics do indeed occur. It has already been acknowledged for the most part that the beginnings of humanity began somewhere on the continent of Africa. However there has been large scale speculation concerning the various human-type individuals which lived in the past based upon skeletal findings particularly fragments of skulls. Upon reconfiguration of the skulls, it has been suggested that they represent a variety of humans but that not all of them represent the so-called Homo sapien or modern human.

In an effort to place the modern human development in Europe, history was being viewed from that context. This understanding would later be replaced with an understanding that the modern human began in Africa. As stated by E. Czable and R. Handler, and A. Lawson, "history is not simply facts strung together to reproduce the past. . ."[2] People often have a motive in reproducing history with a particular viewpoint. Even now there exists two theories, the garden of eden or a weak garden of eden being Africa which is being challenged by a multi-regional evolution of humankind. The point is. Attempts are still being made to separate humans into groups which can be categorized and racially divided. The history of a migration by the modern human out of Africa has all but been overshadowed although "the biological aspects of migration have more to do with the consequences. . ."[3] "Migration and gene flow are important evolutionary factors. Random migration of genes will lead to or promote genetic homoeneity between populations or subpopulations whereas selective migration can promote or maintain differences between populations."[4]

"In human biology there are two virtually independent lines of migration study. (1) Human migration is the mechanism that injects DNA from one gene pool into another. . . (2) Human migration is also the mechanism that inserts similar kinds of individuals into diverse environments. . ."[5] Humans change because of hereditary factors when two mate because of differing DNA. This we witness with every offspring born. However when considering the differing head shapes, facial characteristics, physical stature and even skin color to a degree, it is perhaps that one needs to view the environmental influences occurring through the migration of humans over vast geographical regions. These factors are particularly important because they are not linear in the sense that one can simply follow the path and note the gradual changes. The environmental factors are multiple and varied allowing for a host of differing circumstances even if following a linear path. Subsequently the phenotypic changes may be varied as well allowing for the presentation of similar phenotype characteristics in geographical locations distances from one another. It can not simply be concluded that one group migrated from one point to another a distance away without first considering the environmental factors which may account for the phenotypic characteristics. There is a biological aspect to migration. "When these characteristics appeared in modified form or reduced frequencies, the modifications or less marked occurrences of the traits were arbitrarily ascribed to race mixture."[6] However, "Fishberg (1905) reported that migrants had offspring different in stature from themselves; apparentlly the children had grown up to be different from their parents because of a biological response to the different environment. . .Boas' (1910, 1912) own extensive studies of the results of migration to the United States of Old World Jews and Sicilians is of course, a classic, It demonstrated, as did the studies by others that confirm its findings. . ., that stature and other anthropometric measurements are modified in the offspring of migrants."[7]

The following quotation more than highlights the importance we must give to human variation due to biological influence of migration:

"Baslar (1927) showed that it made a difference to the shape of the head, as measured by the cephalic index, whether an infant had been swaddled and placed on its back or whether it was placed on its side and Ewing (1950) found that migrants who abandoned the practice of swaddling had children who became much narrower headed than themselves. The role of migration in human biology through its moving of DNA from one place to another (in the gametes of migrant individuals) and through subjecting the products of DNA to environments that were effectively different (in the sense that attributes of human organisms are products of DNA) is subject to qualitative differences in human migrations. Migration can be an individual matter, a family matter or a group matter. These and their subtypes have varying biological implilcations."[8]

Many studies have been conducted concerning the anthropometrics of ancient skeletal finds particularly craniometric variations. Efforts have been made to use the differences of these measurements as a basis for racial distinction without having understood or even given consideration to the biological effects of migration. One may appear different as a result of the plasticity in certain phenotypic characteristics but we are still essentially the same having adapted to the environment or having been influenced by the environment. The human species is not one grounded in fixity which would allow one to classify the different groups by race. The plasticity of the human phenotype has allowed the human to respond to a diverse environmental influence. It is for this reason that our ancestors could engage in such a widespread and distant geographical exploration. It is essential to note that it was the one human race who engaged in this exploration and not one particular race. The suggestion that the so-called Negroid African never explores beyond the Sahara desert is ludricious and an insult to human intelligence. In its genesis the human race was a black (pigmented) skinned people. Those who engaged in exploration further and further away from the homeland were likewise black skinned. This is why research in the plasticity with human migration becomes of a greater importance than a false notion, race, which is intended to separate humans into advantage versus disadvantaged categories.

When considering the biological impact of the environment upon the human migration, we must consider such factors as group isolation, gene flow, environmental impact, geographical location, and random/infrequent disruption of an environment such as in the instance of a significant meteor shower, glaciation, earthquakes or volcanic eruptions. Yet one must keep in mind that such environmental influences on the biological aspects of the human are largely external in nature with the exception of blood type causing a microevolutionary change and has absolutely nothing to do with one's intelligence or capacity for learning ruling out the notion of one human being biologically different from another. This idea of one group of humans being superior biologically to another is political nonsense and should be deemed an incorrect notion from its inception in the past. The environment did not effect the brain or the central nervous system nor any other essential organs which make up the one human. We are not dealing with a genetic diversity among the human but rather with morphological and phenotypic diversity among the human resulting from a diverse environmental impact. (Of course the diversity of the environment in distant ancient times was far different from that of today or even in human memory).

Yet we should understand, that although humans demonstrate a plasticity for adapting to the environment. These variations are not so extreme as to suggest classifying humans into subspecies. In fact a recent study by J.H. Relethford shows "that genetic and crania metric data are in agreement, qualitatively and quantitatively, and that there is limited variation in modern humans among major geographic regions."[9] Such variations are more reflective of a microevolutionary change and are insignificant and inappropriate for use in attempts to classify humans in groups. "A variety of data (genetic markers, nuclear DNA, and mitochondrial DNA) all suggest low levels of population differentiation in modern humans, . . . Such low levels of population differentiation imply that the vast majority of genetic variation is among individuals within groups, and not due to variation among groups. As such, these findings show little support for the concept of race or racial classifications."[10] Yet we never consider skin color as a meaningless morphological or phenotypic variation. All humans demonstrate a variation from their original human blackness. Still no human is without this blackness in some degree more or less except perhaps in the case of the albino. Even in the use of the racial language black and white, there are albinos who show deficient or absence of pigmentation. We must understand the nature of our blackness within the context of human variation.

It is interesting to note that even in the instance of human variation. One will find that such variations are not based in the comparison of one group to another but rather in the comparison of one individual to another within a group. The larger human variation was and is found to be in Africa suggesting Africa not only as the site of human origin but as having the greatest variety of differentiating physical features. Were we to use phenotypic characteristics as the basis for race. We would have to begin with Africa and conclude that there are perhaps hundreds of races but in accordance with the true picture, in reality, there is only one human species and variations thereof. "It is thus clear that migration brings into play forces adequate to modify phenotypes appreciably, but the diversity of environments leads to diverse results. . ."[11] K.M. Weiss[12] points out that isolation occurring as a result of distance gives the appearance of genetic barriers but the gene frequency differences are the result of separation by distance or geographical barriers and is not genetic. It is within the confines of isolation that the gene pool available is limited. Hence we should not be surprised that one group begins to look different from another given the environmental impact.

However it is clear that the areas of contention are morphological traits and serological identity which are the seeds of misunderstanding. It is not until we have dealt with these areas that we can begin to see the foolishness of race and the racism which it feeds. We will never see the eras of our ways and the mistakes of the past and present without dissolving ourselves of the burdens of wrong i.e. the misjustice, the social prejudices, the educational deprivation, the use of whiteness or blackness for financial gain performed in the name of race. We need to understand the nature of our blackness because there are no white, black, yellow or red skinned races only human variations. The determination of when someone or when any groups left Africa has been only a smoke screen meant to misdirect the focus of our historical awareness. The question revolves around our likes which are far more than the few dislikes. The question revolves around the question of our human blackness and its variation caused by biological events responding to environmental influences.

While it has been falsely concluded that blood types in serology are an indication of racial types and have been used to suggest racial mixture when certain blood types were present in the so-called colored, Negro, Black or African American, blood types are not determinants of race. During the World War II, blood from African Americans was kept separate from others for that very reason to avoid racial mixture. Although efforts to isolate groups into racial types based on blood grouping, Earnest Hooton in 1931 determined:

"We can make little or nothing of (blood group analysis) from the point of view of racial studies. . . The fact that some of the most physically diverse types of mankind are well nigh indistinguishable from one another in the proportions of the different (alleles), is nigh indistinguishable from one another in the proportions of the different (alleles), is very discouraging. At present it seems that blood groupings are inherited quite independent of any of the physical features whereby we determine race."[13]

Yet Hooton and others like Lawrence Snyder as early as 1925 in knowing "that the ABO system was recognized as a single locus with three major segregation alleles. . ."[14] were disappointed. They had fell in the discovery of truth it seems using scientific inquiry as a front for their racism. It is perhaps that many pursuing scientific investigation seek to conceal their racist agenda behind the purity and professional status of a white lab coat. All the long, the intent had and has been to project one group as being superior to another. Such people fail to see that the ignorance by which they embrace the concept of race taints their ability to investigate the idea truthfully regardless of their credentials. A more recent report titled: "ABO Phenotype and Morphology" by K. Beals, C. Smith and A. Kelso "summaries the geographical distribution of ABO phenotypes. O, A and AB are significantly correlated with latitude, absolute latitude, and longitude."[15] Such occurrence suggest that blood type has been adaptive to environmental impact. Blood type is thus to be considered supportive of human variation and not racial types. This allows us to look more pointedly at morpological traits in the effort to dismantle the race concept.

Those morpological traits used to identify an individual according to race are the nose, lips, eyes, skin color and hair form. Any combination of these traits has been perceived as sufficient by which to classify an individual by race although skin color appears to consistently emerge as the principle determining trait whether it is based on ethnic background or actual skin color. However this difference in skin color is used in determining race and has no basis in fact other than environmental influences. A closer biological examination concerning the coloring of skin will serve as our case in point.

Chapter Six

When discussing human variation, we should note that
". . . skin is not only the largest and most versatile organ of
the body but also with the possible exception of the brain
the most complex."[1] One should expect the greatest adaptation to environmental influences to occur in the skin since
it is exposed to the environment. The skin is composed of
two layers, a dermis and an epidermis.

The epidermis which is the outer layer of the skin is often
referred to as connective tissue. It has a rich supply of blood
and lymph fluids flowing throughout it and contains not only
the hair follicles but the hair, which begin at the inner layer of
the skin, the dermis. Subsequently any environmental influences impacting upon the epidermis might also impact upon
the blood and the hair. The dermis which is the unexposed
layer of the skin lying beneath the epidermis contains the
melanocytes (pigment cells) and is responsible for our skin
color. The epidermis has no color being primarily opaque except for that color being provided primarily by the melanocytes in the dermis. Some other minor contributors of skin
color are the oxyhemoglobin, reduced hemoglobin and the

pigment carotene[2] but the primary pigment produced by the melanocytes is melanin.

Melanin is a black pigment present in all human beings apparently from the dawn of human existence til now with no one being excluded except perhaps the albino. It takes 4 to 6 weeks for this process of coloring to take place from the dermis' multi-layer to the epidermis. This process of skin coloring is thus an ongoing process and is not a one time occurrence which presents a biochemical vulnerability to environmental forces impacting upon the skin.

Some people of the so-called white race have believed that black skin color can be rubbed off. I speak from a personal experience. However skin color is a complex biological process which must be maintained if one's skin color is to be sustained. When exposed to environmental influences changes may occur of a temporary or even of a permanent nature. Yet melanin is a water insoluble pigment which not only does not rub off but nor does it wash out. Then again, it is being continuously produced, similar to the way red blood cells are produced sustaining the color of blood. Stop the flow of red blood cells and one can minorly alter the skin color. Likewise if the skin coloring process were stopped or altered one would realize a significant change in skin color. Skin color is not unalterable in the scheme of human variation. While humans began with dark skin for purposes of photoprotection, certain environmental influences can alter the production of melanin which is responsible for this protection. The skin coloring process could be altered if not irreconcilably disrupted leaving only a back up system intact to respond as a photoprotector (tanning).

Two points are to be considered in understanding skin coloring

1.". . .there are no significant differences in the actual numbers of melanocytes in the skin of different racial groups. The critical factor in the determination of pigmentary variations between and within populations is the melanosome. Microscopic studies of melanosomes in the epidermis of individuals drawn across the skin colour spectrum have demonstrated quantitative and qualitative differences."[3]

2. "There was no genetic discrimination between the two cell types: Caucasoid melanocytes donated melanosomes both to Caucasoid and to Negroid keratinocytes and vice versa (Hirobe, Flynn and Szabo, 1986). In Caucasoid melanocytes - Negroid keratinocyte co-cultures the Caucasoid melanocytes became more dendritic and more pigmented than in Caucasoid melanocyte - Caucasoid keratinocyte co-cultures. This experimental result implies a major feed back mechanism from keratinocytes to melanocytes."[4]

It should be clear from reading above that we are not dealing with different systems as in races but with alterations in the human skin coloring system resulting in variations in intensity of blackness. The human ancestor for us all began with black/brown skin with changes occurring in offspring who migrated distances and encountered environmental influences.

Exposure to certain wavelengths of light can change skin color. "Factors such as UV exposure can alter melanosome configuration."[5] It is the melanosomes contained within the melanocytes which provides the melanin for skin coloring. It is important to note that while skin coloring is an ongoing process. It can be altered given the appropriate environmental impact such as the appropriate wavelength of light.

Assuming the first humans (Homo sapiens) to have been black-skinned as suggested by Lakey and Lewin in 1977,[6] we can best understand that one primary function of the skin is photo-protection. It does this in two ways: 1. The increase melanin present and 2. The thickness of the stratum corneum which is the upper layer of the four in the dermis. The two appear to go hand in hand. When the skin color darkens, the stratum corneum thickens.

This darkening of the skin is provided by a stage 4 melanosome suggesting that our first ancestors had stage 4

71

melanosomes to produce and sustain darkening of the skin for purposes of photo-protection. However, it should be noted that stage 1, 2 and 3 melanosomes exist as well which are smaller and provide a lesser darkening of the skin. Yet the ". . .size of melanosomes per se is neither a distinctive feature of any particular racial group nor necessarily a reflection of the intensity of skin pigmentation."[7] However those displaying the original dark skin coloring can be noted not only to have a dermis which contains mostly large or stage 4 melanosomes that ". . .tend to form 'protective' caps overlying the nuclei. . .more effective resistance to solar radiation damage. . ."[8] The stage 4 melanosomes appear to be front line protectors while the others, stage 1, 2 and 3, appear to be secondary or back-up coming into play when stage 4 melanosomes are disrupted, destroyed or its biological character altered by environmental influences such as certain solar light. We will see later that the nuclei of the melanosomes play a very important role in such alterations. This would leave the smaller stage 1, 2 and 3 melanosomes which are also presesnt in the dark skinned individual but in lesser quantity.

I suggest the stage 1, 2 and 3 melanosomes to be secondary or back-up protectors because when the melanocytes are artificially induced and/or sun tanning is induced, larger melanosomes are produced. It results in a darkening of the skin although only temporarily. It is the large quantity of stage 4 melanosomes which sustains a dark skin coloring. The point is. We should not so easily dismiss the possibility of those cells which make up the skin and having nuclei as their control function from being altered not temporarily as in sun tanning but permanently through environmental events. The front line photo-protector, stage 4 melanosomes, can be shut down or even destroyed given the appropriate environmental stimuli. Human variation in skin color may be genetically or cellularly based but it is caused by the reaction to certain environmental impact.

This environmental impact does not have to be catastrophic nor even obviously noticeable. "Although there was a wide variation in the thickness of the stratum corneum (especially in the Negroid group), there was no significant difference between the mean thickness in Negroids (11.3 um) and that in Caucasoids (9.5 um). A later study (Weigand, Haggood and Gayler, 1974) showed that although the average thickness was almost the same in Negroid and Caucasoid specimens (6.5 um and 7.2 um respectively), the former had more cell-layers and a greater cell density than Caucasoids, suggesting a more compact stratum corneum."[9] The Negroid albino's stratum corneum was similar to that of the Caucasoid albino. The difference is caused by environmental factors not racial differences.

These differences occur as a result of alterations where skin coloring can be inhibited as a result of environmental influences. Biological processes can be affected by the environment. The skin coloring process is a biochemical process. "Tyrosinase is the enzyme responsible for the formation of melanin within the melanosomes. . ."[10] Halprin and Ohkawara (1966) claimed that glutathione was the epidermal substance inhibitory to tyrosinase, and demonstrated that Negroid skin contained less reduced glutathione and less glutathione reductase enzyme than Caucasoid skin (possibly due to genetic differences in the reductase enzyme). This was the first demonstrable biochemical difference between skins of different colours."[11] These are biological differences resulting from environmental impact upon that which protects us, the skin. These are genetic changes/alterations which are mutational in response to the environment and not genetic differences in the sense of suggesting subspecies grouping. Hence skin color variations are in large part a result of environmental stimuli although not as simple as being determined by geographical location only. This permanent response to environmental stimuli which can further be passed on to one's offsprings was a biological mutation of the skin coloring system. It should be further noted:

"A major structural difference between the two skins is that black skin has notably fewer elastic fibers every-

73

where than does white skin, whether or not there has been sun exposure. In addition, the architecture of the subepidermal oxytalan and elaumin fibers is very different in the two skins, and particularly in the face."[12]

"The presence of elastic fibers in the face and other exposed skin areas is one of the key indices of dermal photodamage in white skin."[13]

It is clear that the sun can be an environmental factor having had impact upon the skin even to the extent of damaging it when the skin was suppose to protect given certain circumstances. What we witness today is a premature wrinkling of skin which has been largely depigmented except in the instance of temporary sun tanning. Is this structural damage resulting from an environmental impact involving the sun's radiation. So-called white skin reportedly has an elasticity in the epidermis which is largely absent in the black skin. One might expect premature wrinkling in skin where an abundant presence of previous elasticity decreased. The question is whether or not the increase presence of this elasticity is in response to structural damage making it a genetic mutational response to an environmental stimuli. Assuming the so-called initial modern humans to have had black skin, one could use the presence of structures in that skin to be the norm. Any changes or absence of structures in the skin would suggest genetic mutational responses to environmental stimuli.

"There are more apocrine glands in the face and scalp of Blacks than whites. . . In the few specimens we have of black axillary skin, we found some mucous glands; in the many axillary skin specimens of white people we never found mucous glands."[14]

"Black skin everywhere has a thick and compact dermis. There are islands of an intermediate layer in the dermis of the face, a layer which is very distinct in the facial skin of white women. . . A characteristic feature

74

of black skin dermis is the close stacking of the collagenous fiber bundles in the reticularis dermis in black skin are smaller than those found in white skin."[15]

"A peculiarity of black skin is the presence of many collagenous fiber fragments in the dermal interstices. . ."[16]

As we all know, the skin of a white skin boxer tears and injures far easier than that of a black skin boxer. The same is evident in the aged. Further differences indicated by W. Montague in black versus white skin suggest that the so-called whited skin has indeed been structurally damaged and genetically mutated when acknowledging the skin of the modern human in their origin to have been black. These differences are:

1. "Regardless of age, black skin appears to have more superficial vessels than white skin. . .black skin always contains many large, dilated lymph vessels everywhere, particularly on the face, regardless of age."[17]

2. "There are many myelinated nerves and nerve endings in the dermis of black facial skin."[18]

3. ". . .black skin is smoother and firmer than white skin."[19]

4. "In black skin, characterized by a low level of sulfhydryl compounds, tyrosinase-catalyzed oxidation of tyrosine leads to dopaquinone which is largely converted to dopachrome and then to melanin. In white nonirradiated skin, with a relatively high sulfhydryl content, most of the enzymically generated dopaquinone is converted to glutathionyldopas, so that little or no dopachrome, and therefore melanin, is formed. . . Thus we could now say that the striking difference in pigmentary color is the result of genetic difference in cutaneous levels of GSH rather than in the types of melanocytes. We believe that this may provide an entry to-

ward the understanding of the unique biological properties of black skin that are apparently lacking in white
skin."[20]

5. "This implies the existence of a biochemical
mechanism that turns up or down the amount of melanin in black or white skin, respecitively."[21]
The pseudo-scientific definition of race used today by all of
us ignores such scientific findings.

We have all heard of sun tanning, a process in which skin
pigmentation or darkening increases in response to the skin's
exposure to ultraviolet radiation given off by the sun. This is a
common practice by those whose skin has a significant reduction in its blackness. Such wavelengths of solar energy can
temporarily alter or stimulate the increase production of melanin resulting in a temporary darkening of the skin or in the
instance of over exposure can burn the skin when the blackness of the skin is inadequate to protect it. The biological
changes in the skin coloring is directly in response to various
solar wavelengths. They are ultraviolet A, ultraviolet B, ultraviolet C, Vacuum ultraviolet, x-rays, gamma rays and cosmic
rays. While it has been suggested that all wavelengths below
ultraviolet B be excluded because the earth's ozone prevents
them from entering the earth's atmosphere limiting their environmental impact, we must keep in mind that the ozone
layer can be depleted and holes can be punched through it as
a result of cataclizmic events.

Exposure to such wavelength radiation normally pre-
vented from entering earth's atmosphere would not only
cause an increase in skin cancer but biological changes in
the skin coloring system if the filtration of such wavelengths
has broken down. Normally, "melanin protects against damaging UV by scattering, by absorption of radiant energy,
and by the dissipation of this energy as heat."[22] I should
mention that other environmental factors play a role although the role may be less when not in combination with
radiation. Those environmental factors are altitude, humid-
ity, latitude and/or temperature. In fact it appears that some

morphological characteristics such as in the nose shape may be in response to such environmental influences. Yet geographical clining of skin color does not account for genetic mutational changes in groups simultaneously exposed to the same intense environmental factors. It is the variation in the intensity of the environmental factors that account for these variations in skin color. Significant depigmentation does not permanently occur simply because of distant geographical relocation into areas where ultraviolet intensity is less. I would suggest that spontaneous events or short term significant events occurred in earth's history resulting in environmental factors in some geographical locations of a sufficient magnitude to result in genetic mutations. If the melanin pigmentation was not enough to fend off the impact of an external stimuli, "radiation, trauma, contusion, and a number of other insults cause alterations in skin pigmentation."[23]

"As far back as the Upper Paleolithic period (5,000 to 10,000 years ago, a period characterized by stone implements) no racial divisions appear to have developed. If a new mutation might be expected to spread about 50 kilometers in 100 generations, to travel the distance of 10,000 km from China to France would have required some 400,000 years. . ."[24] Understanding the modern human can only be dated back approximately 100,000 to 200,000 years ago on the continent of Africa and only 30,000 to 40,000 years ago in Europe and Asia suggest that no natural occurring mutation such as by natural selection has taken place. Between this 30,000 to 40,000 years ago and the Paleolithic period of 5,000 to 10,000 years ago something more dramatic and perhaps nearly spontaneous took place in some but not all environments as groups of humans split off during the many migrations. Suddenly there were contrasting differences which society has come to falsely recognize as racial divisions because of the phenotype changes. This is further supported by the fact that not all human groups migrating encountered this change such as the aborigine of Australia who are believed to have migrated through Asia to their home in Australia. They remained black skinned suggesting the changes to have been more spontaneous rather than a long drawn out event. (see "Genetic Relationships of Europeans, Asians, and Africans and the Origin of Modern Homo Sapiens" by Masatoski Nei and Gregory Livshihts and "Genetic and Fossil Evidence for the Origin of Modern Humans" by C.B. Stringer and P. Andrews).

Recognizing such a time factor, an event which might cause mutation to take place would be one avenue to be explored in understanding how one group might lose the stage 4 melanosomes or the ability to produce a sustained dark skin coloring except on a temporary basis. It appears that the ability to produce this sustained darkening of the skin was damaged. It is unlikely that environmental circumstances like that found today around the world could cause such changes or we would be witnessing such events today. Some event or events occurred in the past to change the skin of some permanently. Obviously given the reoccurrence of these environmental events it could occur today as well.

In fact, "shortly after the birth of genetics, investigators recognized that gene mutations may occur spontaneously in nature. The word 'spontaneously' does not necessarily mean that these mutations are always the result of more chance; it means that these mutations could be the result of chance or could be produced by some external environmental agents existing in nature, which we are not always able to identify. Geneticists believe that the few or many alleles of the same gene found in the genetic pool of a species arose as a consequence of several spontaneous mutations of an original gene, which occurred during the long existence of the species."[25]

When studying the biological response of the skin's coloring, we will need to consider not only the cell but the cellular structure and how these cell structures respond to environmental influences. While the production of melanin is a biochemical/biological process, its function or action is directly in response to genetic altering events and/

or hormonal influences or the lack thereof in skin cells. Since the genetic response is a chemical one, it can be subjected to internal hormonal or external stimuli i.e. solar radiation influences. For example if the enzyme L-tyrosine is altered, the production of melanin will likewise be altered because the tyrosinae activity is necessary if melanin is to be produced. Genetic modifications of this enzyme alone by means of external stimuli or by external stimuli facilitating or inhibiting other internal controls acting upon this enzyme can result in permanent changes of the melanosomes being produced. Whereas one may have had stage 4 melanosomes before, the impact of a stimuli upon the tyrosinae enzyme may result now mostly in the production of stage 1, 2 melanosomes giving one the appearance of being white. "There are a number of controls that may act at various epigenetic levels, such as transcription, translation, and post-translational modification of the enzyme such as glycosylation, and controls affecting the vesicular routing of the product as well as mechanisms affecting the rate of aggregation of premelanosomes. . . Clearly, all these are points at which skin pigmentation can be influenced. . ., the simplest mutation can lead to dramatic changes in the phenotype of the individual."[26]

While the skin may be tough structurally, its process of pigmentation is a sensitive one given exposure to impacting external stimuli. "Experiments on pigmentation genes in mice which are similar in its response to that of the human pigmentation gene have shown over 150 different mutations possible."[27] These mutations are at the genetic level and thus become permanent. Such changes are not temporary responses to routine weather conditions as in suntanning because of temperature increases. Further, "these mutations affect visible hair and eye color, typically in a uniform manner, by affecting mechanisms involved in, but not restricted to, melanocyte function."[28] The notion of blond hair and blue eyes are not phenotypic characteristics depicting someone of the white race but instead are mutational responses to an environmental influence impacting upon the physical appearance of the human who was and whose ancestors were initially black skinned.

To adequately understand the skin in its potential for variation in skin color, one must look beyond simply the physical appearance i.e. skin color to its underlying causes. It is not a question of what race one is but rather a question of the skin's cellular function in the production of melanin. Melanin is a product of the biological events taking place within cells of which the skin is composed of. To be more specific all functions of the cell are dictated by its nucleus. This nucleus contains chromosomes which are composed of genes made up of DNA, a chemical. Accordingly, the cell's function can be altered within by changes within the nucleus. Then since all of these functions are chemical in nature, the functions dictated by the nucleus can also be determined by enzyme activities which influences the cell and its nucleus inhibiting or facilitating an action. Any change therefore in the action of the enzyme can thus also alter the cell function. In either situation an external stimuli may impact upon both.

There are many ways for skin color to be altered especially since it is a biological process which is continually ongoing. The external stimuli to which I am referring as the primary cause of skin cell function alteration is that of the energy from radiation. "It is the energy that gives rise to the biological changes. . ."[29] The impact of such energy upon the skin is made easy because the nucleus of the cell is the most radiosensitive as is the skin. This is important when understanding that the nucleus is responsible for the cell's function such as the variations in skin color. Thus the lack of or decrease in pigmentation in the so-called white person is not a result of a lack of ultraviolet A, B or blockage of sunlight limiting the skin's photo-protection ability. Rather it is a result of radiation energies causing alterations in skin cell function. "Mammalian cells are 500 to 1000 times more susceptible to damage induced by ionizing radiation than to that caused by UV. . ."[30]

The impact of radiation energy upon the cell particularly the nucleus' chromosomes or genes is called a mutation. "The term mutation is defined as a hereditary alteration."[31] These alterations become not only permanent but nonreversible and will be passed from generation to generation by way of genetics. The types of mutation which occurs in this instance most often are point mutations but other types of impacting mutations which can occur although less often are chromosome aberration and splice-site mutations. Once this mutation occurs and has had several cell generations, this mutant cell will have established itself as the new norm becoming undetectable. This mutant cell becomes the origin of a new phenotype giving rise to variations in human physical characteristics such as skin color, hair type, and eye color. The variations are dependent upon the impact of this external stimuli if any at all because I would conclude that not all of our ancestral human family was exposed (with some being exposed less than others and while some would certainly have been exposed fatally). We should understand that not all exposures to radiation is lethal or negative or even therapeutic but can also be the cause of alterating mutations resulting in morphological and phenotypical changes. "Painter suggest that there are alterations induced in DNA by radiations which the mammalian cell has not encountered frequently in its evolutionary history. His conclusion retains something of the viewpoint of earlier decades: 'certain kinds of lesions formed in mammalian DNA by ionizing radiation' 'have little' or no probability of being repaired."[32] Once again understanding all humans to have a black-skinned ancestral history, any mutational or biological alterations effecting skin color would be permanent.

One would think that such changes or mutations would be obvious to simple observations perhaps microscopically. However any such mutated gene, chromosome or cell having undergone multiple generation regeneration appear as normal or original but has experienced a mutational alteration. "Point mutations are molecular alterations of genes not accompanied by visible aberrations. . . The immediate result of mutations is that the cells are incapable of performing some vital biochemical reactions."[33] The production of melanin is one such vitally important biochemical reaction because skin coloring is necessary for photoprotection. The absence or decrease in this biochemical reaction suggest that mutational alterations has indeed occurred in those lacking adequate melanin production for such photoprotection, one of the basic functions of human skin. We should understand that initially all our ancestors were black skinned. Our skin is the front line barrier to impacting environmental elements such as radiation. If changes are going to occur, it seems reasonable to expect it in the skin first. It appears that only the skin has changed dispelling ideas of superior/inferior based in the concept race. Yet science and our educational system has been reluctant or negligent to inform us of this fact allowing a pseudo idea like race to be fostered and perpetuated.

There are differences in our skin but this can best be explained by these mutational alterations which resulted in chromosome strands having been repaired to their original state in appearance but with new instructional guidelines having been imposed by the effects of certain radiations. It became just as sound as the original chromosome and multiplied because of population isolation.

Chapter Seven

Groups of humans were separated by natural barriers such as lakes, rivers, mountains and distance because of migration. Intra-group breeding would have taken place. Any changes which occurred to one generation is now many and would continue unless the group was subjected to other environmental stimuli which caused further variations/alterations. It can never go back to being the same. Yet I stress the point that these phenotypical and morphological changes resulting from such skin cell function alteration involves the external body only changing only one's appearance. The brain does not have the radiosensitivity of the skin. Differences here are more the result of images having been associated with skin color and other phenotype characteristics and the classification of such descriptions in racial categories. It is more a result of social climate not discounting society's ignorance rather than having any significant genetic basis. Under this variation in skin color, people are the same. We simply need to understand this and rid the human race of their false perception that we live in a multi-racial world. This is the big lie which has become the foundation of much of the world's hate, oppression, genocide, enslavement and division. It is time to change this equation that we are different but equal because such an equation can never sum up to being equal. We are desperately in need, nationwide to world-wide, of discussion and resolution on the misrepresentation of race and its impact upon national and world politics.

We can begin this discussion by assessing how it is that part of our human race experienced environmental stimuli sufficient to result in mutations, which are a variation in hereditary factors. Considering the fact that dark skin was not only first but an essential for photo-protection, any large scale changes therein should be viewed as a mutation. In The Biochemical Genetics of Man, it states:

"If a mutation occurs at a sufficiently sensitive site within the amino acid sequences of a protein it may well abolish function completely. Such mutant proteins will then have to be recognized by methods which are independent of their biological function. . . It is obviously possible for a protein to suffer a mutation so destructive that both biological function and antigenic function are abolished."[1]

"Most mutations which can be recognized at a molecular level involve some impairment of protein function. Among the enzymes of intermediary metabolism, where genetic defects have been most extensively studied, mutation usually results in a large reduction but not complete abolition of enzymatic activity."[2]

"In general, however, mutations tend to lead to reduced enzyme activity with impairment of cellular function. . If the enzyme is part of a multi-enzyme complex impairment of function in one enzyme can appear to affect all the components of the complex. . ."[3]

In so-called white skin, there is obviously a significant reduction in the skin's ability to produce the melanin needed for continuous skin coloring although this function is not completely absent. On the other hand there are not only reductions in certain functions of the skin cells but there are some functions which appear to be absent or in the instance of mutation abolished. Examination of white skin has found it not only to have a reduction of the presence of apocrine glands in the face and scalp when compared to black skin but further yet mucous glands observed in the axillary of skin which is black but absent or abolished in white skin. These differences along with others would seem to support the incident of mutation accounting for this hereditible variation. Looking backwards from white to black skin, we get a glimpse of not only what the original was and is but also an understanding of the mutations which have taken place as a result of contact with certain environmental stimuli, certain types of radiation exposure to large groups of humans who were initially dark skin or black skinned.

We should note that there are more than 50 gene loci or sites in the human skin genetic chain where mutations can directly or indirectly reduce the skin's pigmentation by altering the function of the melanocyte. The alterations which occur here are hereditary. These loci are points within the chromosome providing specific hereditary characters to the offspring. When this reduction occurs in the production of melanin, other skin pigments may dominate although they do not have the photoprotection qualities of melanin. These are oxyhemoglobin which is oxygenated blood coming to the skin surface, reduced hemoglobin which is venous blood in the skin tissue, carotene which is a yellowish pigment from fatty-rich areas and melanoid. This clearly presents a large range of option in skin color variations when melanin is significantly reduced. However the differences are quantitative and not qualitative. In other words there is no such concept as racial types except in the socio-political arena and it has no basis in what is real.

Rather than trying to determine when humans separated with this hidden agenda to justify racial classification, the focus of research and teaching should be on determining when and how did these mutations which account for hereditible phenotype variations occur. The only evolutionary process to have occurred among this modern human out of Africa has been micro-evolutionary in nature ruling out the possibility of the development of subspecies. This has been further substantiated by the fact that all humans are "completely fertile in cross matings. . ."[4] Even "ABO blood groups are quantitative: that is, similar alleles are present in virtually all populations, but the frequencies vary. And we must remember that most genes appear to be identical in all human beings."[5] Then it is clear as stated earlier not only was our human ancestors black skinned. Even those who migrated out of Africa to various distant locations remained black skinned until a relatively recent time period in history. Certain groups in certain locations would have been subjected to the exposure of environmental stimuli which may have been detrimental to some while causing mutation or alteration in skin cell function in others. These groups of humans from that point in prehistory forward experienced reductions and abolition in skin cell function. "Mutations that occur in a functional region of a chromosome are apt to diminish the activity of the gene product, quantitatively and qualitatively, that is associated with that locus. . . Mutation may occur spontaneously. . ."[6] And they are irreversible. It should not be surprising that some humans have type B, C melanosomes and few type A although having a similar quantity of melanocytes. This resulted in skin variations which could be transmitted from generation to generation of offspring. Hence from that point forward the appearance of some humans' skin color was changed forever.

"The fact that Radiation, trauma, contusion, and a number of other insults cause alterations in skin pigmentation. . .is testimony to the intricacies that surround the phenomenon of skin coloration."[7] However only one of the factors should be of great interest in understanding the nature of our blackness. That is radiation because of the radio-sensitivity of the human skin making it prone to phenotype changes. Such changes would occur nearly spontaneously and become hereditible in the offsprings. To be more specific the type of radiation of which I refer is called ionizing radiation.

Although it is plausible and even probable given human migration and exposure to adverse environmental stimuli, no human or group of humans are known to have been exposed to ionizing radiation. But then we have never considered looking beyond race to explain human skin color variations and phenotype characteristics within this context. "Some mutation react in a favorable way to a changed environment and in this way increase the possibilities of the population. . . It is, I consider, fairly evident that mutations with major or even drastic phenotypic effects play an essential role in evolution."[8] Through experimental testing with mice, of which results would be compatible with human skin exposure, germ cell mutations and chromosome aberrations occurring from ionizing radiation can induce genetic damage and/or alterations which are hereditary. The result of such mutations become hereditary because groups experiencing such phenotype variations were isolated by natural geographical barriers. The reduced gene flow preventing separate groups from interbreeding for long periods concluding in similarities within the group and differences outside the group from the perspective of one's physical appearance. Hence these phenotype variations are then passed on to each generation as the new norm. The result can be so-called white skin, blue eyes, blond hair as the new norm although the original norm may have been blackk/brown skin, brown eyes, tightly curled hair. The mutation or chromosome aberration caused by the ionizing radiation can cause such seemingly dramatic phenotype changes almost instantaneously and certainly irreversibly to be passed on from generation to generation. We can refer to such mutational variations as microevolution.

The area being impacted upon is primarily the skin because of its sensitivity to radiation exposure. However it should be noted that ultraviolet radiation exposure which can produce first and second degree skin burns is insufficient to cause the needed mutational changes for phenotype variations to occur. While controlled or limited ultraviolet exposure can cause a temporary darkening of the skin by stimulating the production of melanin as a protective response, such temporary skin darkening is not a mutation. Ionizing radiation which would be an unusual environmental occurence is needed to facilitate genetic mutations and chromosome aberrations which result in phenotype variations. "Ionizing rays are so called because their principals means of dissipation of energy in passage through matter is the ejection of electrons from atoms in their path. When an electrically neutral atom has lost one or more of its orbital electrons, the atom is left positively charged, that is, ionized. An ionized atom is one eager for chemical reaction."[9] The action of the skin cell and its nucleus is a chemical reaction. Upon being ionized, it is in a state of readiness for alteration because of chromosome breakage and DNA breaks and unless it repairs the damage done identically, cross linking, alterations or mutations will take place producing a different but sound DNA replacement and become irrevocable. "The DNA changes that occur with mutation are very limited: Nucleotides may be substituted, deleted, or added. The effects on gene function are quite varied and complex, depending on the location of these events within the gene or its regulatory sequences."[10] "A few radiologically produced cross-links can alter profoundly the physical and mechanical properties of the irradiated. . ."[11]

The process of ionizing is random and is not selective to any particular areas (molecule or atom) exposed to it. Thus the results are random, indiscriminate, and unpredictable. It is impossible to determine what the results or variations may be until the process is complete. There can be a whole host of differing phenotype appearances. The one which will persist in following generations are dependent upon gene flow, selection and genetic drift.

The skin unlike the connective tissue, muscle, bone or tissue of ectodermal origin i.e. the central nerve system, sense organs or adrenal medulla has a greater sensitivity to ionizing radiation. It is thus more subject to mutational variation. One should therefore expect to see variation in skin color but no mutated alterations in the bone structure, the connective tissues and muscles attached nor any changes in the nerves i.e. the brain. Subsequently we remain one species and not a group of subspecies. Then the skin is not only more sensitive but it is classified as a progenitive tissue meaning that changes or alterations in skin color can be given to the offspring. It has been suggested "that there are alterations induced in DNA by radiations which the mammalian cell has not encountered frequently in its evolutionary history."[12] Hence those groups who experienced variations in phenotype as a result of ionizing radiation exposure in that environment became the progenitor. They are the biologically related ancestors from whom all the variations in skin color were derived and inherited.

The skin is influenced by this ionization process because it is the front line defense of the body. The ionization process occurs mostly in a water base. "Many human tissues are made up of 70-80% water. Thus, we identify water as the most probable material in which the ionizations caused by radiation may occur. The resulting chemical products may react with biologically important organic molecules and thus be indirectly responsible for an observable effect."[13] The production of melanin in one such important biological function which if altered would result in an observable affect of changes in the skin color. Obviously the skin is composed largely of water. The primary solvent of the skin cells' molecules including its nucleic acids and enzyme is water suggesting that the biological processes occur in a water solvent which can be ionized.

Hence skin sensitivity is further recognized because of its biologic macromolecules. Such long chain molecules easily absorb high energy radiations such as ionizing radiation. Macromolecules are important for metabolic activity and for hereditary traits passing from generation to the next. The exposure of the skin's macromolecules to this ionization process can result in physical changes and/or changes in the physicochemical functions in skin cells. These changes (even minor ones) can be due to an enzyme having been inactivated or altered chemically preventing a catalytic activity needed to inhibit or facilitate a cell function or parts thereof. Alterations can also occur in the chemical activity of the cell nucleus itself, chromosome breakage or in cross linking.

Then not only is the skin vulnerable to ionizing radiation because of its water composition and chain molecules. Perhaps most important of all, the area of greatest radiosensitivity in any living tissue is its cells' nucleus. The nucleus not only controls the action of the cell but contains those chromosomes and genes which determines how we appear and what we will look like as concerns the color of our skin, eyes and hair type/color. Because of cell division, it is these characteristics which will be replicated and passed on to the next generation of offspring. It is here within the nucleus that ionization can cause chromosome breakage, mutations, cross linking and effect repairs where errors in replication can occur resulting in the visible changes such as the skin changes and skin color variations we witness today.

Some refer to such differences as having resulted from geographical clining. Clining does occur with distant relocating being influenced by ultraviolet radiation exposure combined with such factors as latitude, altitude, snow, clouds and other frequent environmental situations. However such influences are minimal and would change with further movements over great distances. It must be recognized that while groups of humans can be exposed to similar environments, the random impact of this ionization process upon the many possible loci of the chromosome can determine a variety of results. It would further depend upon the amount of ionizing radiation exposure. It is this process which is responsible for the variations in hereditary phenotype.

While I noted earlier that ultraviolet radiation can cause

excitation resulting in temporary increase in skin coloring, this ionization process becomes irreversible and does not result in increase skin coloring but less as a result of mutations and chemical reactions. In fact "mammalian cells are 500 to 1000 times susceptible to damage induced by ionizing radiation than to that caused by UV. . ."[14] I would suggest that such exposure was random and infrequent occurring more or less in some areas to barely if any in others, although it must be acknowledged that some variations have resulted from genetic drift. However recognizing that the first humans were black skinned to cope with the environment, it was the ionization process which resulted in the hereditary mutations which caused the significant changes in melanin production and morphological changes to even variations in the blood groups to be passed on to the offspring of some groups. Thus we have what some wrongly insist upon calling major racial groups such as Negroid, Caucasoid and Mongoloid, terms which are misleading to deceptive when seeking to understand the human and the nature of our blackness. We are all black but only in variations because of the alterations and mutations caused by this ionization process. There is no such thing as a white person, a red person, a yellow person only variations in one's blackness allowing secondary skin coloring to become more manifest although the melanocyte has the primary function of skin coloring. It is in this sense that all humans today are literally shades of black .

This ionization process is caused by exposure to radiation. While radiation is a natural and continuously occurring phenomenon in the environment to which nearly everyone is exposed, it is not any and all radiation which can cause mutation. Ionizing radiation in particular is required to the extent that it can cause biological changes. Such ionizing radiation would have occurred randomly and with variations in the effectual intensity. Ionized radiation is a product of eletro magnetic energy produced by cosmic rays, gamma rays, x-rays and heavy particles energy. Chromosomes hit by these ions can break. It is the absorption of this ionizing energy by the skin that resulted in the biological changes inhibiting the production of melanin. The result was the establishment of variations in new norms for skin color in those groups of humans exposed. Other areas impacted upon (not to mention possible morphological changes) were the hair, sebaceous glands, sweat glands and endothelium which are all found in the basal layer of the skin's epidermis.[15] It is important to note that the epidermis or outer layer of the skin which is composed of collagen and elastic is resistive to change unless subject to a very intense exposure. Subsequently with changes in the epidermis diminishing the production of the melanin, the heavy supply of blood channelling throughout the epidermis provides for skin coloring. This is the so-called white person. The black/brown melanin is there only significantly reduced by the effect of this ionization process. Unlike suntanning, it is irrevocable.

The sun is the source of much of the natural occurring radiation providing a constant exposure. It would appear unlikely that such exposure is responsible for the alteration/mutation unless unusual events took place on the sun. The environmental impact responsible for the changes in human skin color was a random and perhaps fading occurrence limiting to alleviating its replication today. This ionizing biological alteration/mutation would be an event or events which occurred in earth's history. The solar radiation to which the earth has been subjected to day in and day out since early times does in fact have potentially harmful radiation but in the normal scenario much of the sun's harmful rays are being filtered out by the earth's ozone layer. Hence the events which would allow for this ionizing radiation exposure was a unique and seldom occurrence much of which has dissipated with the passage of time.

It is well known that the earth earlier on has had a violet history with volcanoes, earthquakes, large and mulitple meteorite strikes and other extraterrestial events impacting upon the earth and its environment. The events were random and sporadic. Perhaps even more importantly, such events were limited occurring more so in certain geographical locations than others in which humans lived. These events had the potential to produce ionizing radiation of an intensity sufficient to cause biological changes in the skin of those human groups exposed.

A recent example demostrates not only the random occurrence of ionization caused by cosmic rays but its disruptive potential in an environment as well. On February 23, 1956[16] the influence of cosmic rays upon the ionosphere resulted in a disruption of short wave radio connection. It was associated with a solar burst although cosmic ray origins are not fully understood only that they occur within the galaxy and not necessarily within the solar system. "Possible energetic sources of cosmic rays in the galaxy include: supernovae explosions, pulsars, and the galactic nucleus, which may contain a black hole. . . There exist sources of high energy particles inside the supercluster and beyond which are not obviously present in our own galaxy. These include radio galaxies, N-galaxies, and quasars. . . Some of these ejected particles may reach our galaxy and be observed by us on earth."[17] The ionization produced during this Feb. 23 event indicated above had impact upon both the high and low latitudes although it is known that ionization has a greater impact in higher latitudes and altitudes. In fact in the example mentioned above, "a second 'late' type of anomalous ionization started much more gradually, reached its maximum only some hours after the solar burst and lasted several days. This type of anomalous ionization showed a high degree of isotropy and has been observed at geomagnetic latitudes above 70° only."[18] The areas impacted upon can be restricted when considering this ionization process. One should then expect the greater human exposure to have occurred outside of Africa. Further one should expect those in the higher latitudes and even altitudes to have a less melanin production resulting from the impact of biological altering ionization upon the skin. We do witness in general such skin color variations from dark to light as one goes further from the equator but not because of clining nor exposure to UV rays. Obviously there are exceptions for reasons sited earlier.

Yet cosmic rays are not the only source of ionizing radiation which can effect human skin color. Gamma rays and x-rays also emit ionizing radiation. Direct cosmic ray exposure is only one scenario of significant impact upon the environment. Irradiated meteorites from exposure to cosmic rays plummeted to earth subjecting vast areas to irradiated interplanetary dust and irradiated meteorites. Humans could potentially have been exposed to ionizing radiation emitted from such sources. An understanding of where the greater number of meteorites or asteroids impacted earth would be of benefit to detemine the significance of this source of ionizing radiation. The eruptive activity of the many large volcanoes now extinct are believed to have not only facilitated biological diversity but new species as well having been caused by atomic isotopes being exposed to the earth's surface and atmosphere. Such radioactive materials would have emitted the ionizing radiation of gamma rays. Currently no active volcano even approaches the magnitude of those extinct volcanoes. Interestingly enough one such extinct site was found to be in the higher latitudes near Norway. "The spasms of eruptive activity associated with such rapid outpourings of lava may have substantially affected the chemistry and circulation of the oceans and atmosphere."[19] This would have had an impact on the evolution of life and possibly the micro-evolutions of humans exposed who survived not only the catastrophic trauma but the radiation exposure. The radioactive materials being exposed would have decayed over a prolonged period of time causing exposure to become less threatening with time. Subsequently any exposure to mutating ionizing radiation then would be less of a threat today. The radioactive decay has reduced. Clearly the environmental conditions of those ancient times would and did differ from current times. We have not experienced any significant asteroid, comet or meteorite impacts in populated area today as occurred in the Paleolithic time period.

Interestingly humans not only existed then but had migrated to Europe. It is in these higher latitudes that human groups would be exposed to ionizing radiation produced by such asteroid, comet and meteorite impacts with earth. It appears that such events were of greater occurence outside of Africa even the volcanic eruptions and earthquakes precipitated by such impacts.

The same radiation exposure was possible during human cave dwelling. Those human groups who left Africa encountered the climatic conditions of an ice age which lasted up until approximately 10,000 years ago. The harsh conditions of this ice age in Europe required these human groups to dwell in caves. Cave dwellings were potential areas of exposure to natural terrestial decaying radioactive substances such as "Uranium, Thorium, Actinium an isotope of Potassium and an isotope of Rubidium."[20] Waves of gamma radiation would have been emitted from such sources. The energy absorbed by the skin from these gamma rays collide with random loci of the genes which make up the chromosomes of the skin cells. The result is a genetic alteration or mutation causing variations in chemical or biological functions in the skin which is living tissue. This is how the process of ionization works and gamma rays are an ionizing radiation. Of course exposure would have occurred at a sublethal level as not to destroy the skin tissue or kill the human being. It is the atom of which all living tissue is composed that is ionized.

"As atoms are generally parts of molecules, ionization may thus produce negatively charged and positively charged molecules, called free radicals. The latter have an extremely high chemical reactivity and will rapidly undergo further changes. New substances, of a completely different nature, may be formed in this way, and the changes will be the greater the more intense is the irradiation.

If such a phenomena affects the tissues of living creatures, dramatic changes may occur, with far-reaching results"[21]

Chromosomes which contain the duplicating material for duplicate cell reproduction and offsprings is composed of these atoms.

"If, for any reason, the chromosomes are disturbed by some external agency, an abrupt change may take place in the nature of living species, and the offspring may show characteristics which differ greatly from their ancestors. Such a change is known as a mutation.

Often the result of a mutation is a freak and the mutant is unable to survive and dies out. But, if mutant propagates with the newly acquired characteristics, a new species (or new variant) may be evolved.

Radiations passing through cells produce ionization and break up molecules. . . This produces chemical changes in the cells which may be lethal or affect their properties. . .

Only irradiation of the germ cell (ovum, sperm, seeds) can give rise to mutation."[22]

The human skin as pointed out earlier on is sensitive to such radiation exposure. This exposure is without question the cause of our external variations in appearance. Once again the old adage is appropriate: 'Beauty is only skin deep.' Likewise our differences are only skin deep as a result of the events which have been discussed. Obviously it is my hope that we begin to explore more so our likes than our dislikes and that we further research these events to better understand the nature of our blackness.

This scenario explained above warrants further understanding from a theoretical view. What ever events took place to produce the ionization which caused these mutations in skin color production was a seldom occurring event. It can happen again only if given the right circumstances of events. While the exact cause may remain largely unknown,

96

some theories have been postulated as a potential source of this ionization. It is simply that up until now. We have been so caught up with the socio-political-religious western world views on race. We have not only ignored the scientific advancements discarding the concept, race, but we have further been short sighted in our efforts to determine how, why, when and where environmental and/or atmospheric events occurred causing the radiation of melanin along with other superficial skin changes in some while not in others at least not to the same degree.

The first evidence of this theory was discovered in ice cores taken from the Antarctic. "In analysis of NO_3 in an Antarctic ice core we have found four spikes of high concentrations, three of which occur at depths which correspond roughly to the dates of known galactic supernovae."[23] I emphasize known supernovae. The high concentration is that of x-rays and gamma rays produced from a supernovae explosion. The energy produced has been suggested to be in the form of photons. "Most of the energy of the photons would ultimately be deposited in the atmosphere in the form of ionizations."[24] It is the process of ionization which can cause genetic mutations resulting in biochemical alterations in the skin's ability to produce melanin. The energy level of these x-rays and gamma rays reaching earth's atmosphere from such supernovae explosions were sufficiently high to have a biological impact on human skin.

For a supernovae explosion to have this impact without the energy level dissipating before reaching earth's atmosphere, it would have had to occurred nearby. "Such a SNE may be expected to occur within a few tens of light years of our Solar System once every hundred million years or so. A short Y-ray pulse of this magnitude would. . .directly affect the terrestrial atmosphere in ways that can be important for surface life. . . This radiation could. . .have occurred over an interval as long as a year. . ."[25] Even though the earth's atmosphere would initially protect surface life from exposure to extraterrestial radiation, "effects on the surface would be indirect, such as those resulting from NO production and subsequent O_3 destruction."[26] With the destruction or depletion to the ozone layer not only will ionized matter which can linger in the gravitational field of earth 10 years or greater settle to earth as it penetrated the depleted shield of earth's atmosphere but lethal dosages of ultraviolet C would also reach the earth's surface. The result is a modification of the immediate environment for a period of time from the exposure which can cause the biological impact on humans living on or near that surface.

This supernovae explosions not only produced the ionization which was responsible for the biochemical alteration in melanin production but may have been responsible for initiating the ice age. As we well know, there were humans living in or near the areas enveloped by or experiencing climatic influences of that ice age. It would have been at this time that humans who were initially black skinned experienced biochemical alterations of their skin's melanin production from exposure to the ionization not the cold. It was not the adaptation to climate referred to as clining which accounts for skin variations which can be passed on to offsprings but rather the exposure to ionized materials for an extended period.

In fact the theory suggest that this extraterrestrial ionized material was responsible for initiating the ice age by depleting the ozone layer. The depletion of the ozone layer is one possible rationale for the cooling of earth's climate. While the ozone depletion would have been a temporary one, the ionization impacting earth's stratosphere would also have been intense "over 300 times more ionization than caused by normal cosmic rays in an entire year."[27] This sudden surge of impacting ions which can cause biochemical alterations and affect terrestrial life is fortunately a seldom occurring event. This is all the more reason why I must emphasize. The event was of sufficient ionized energy and for a sufficiently prolonged period of time to biologically alter the skin's melanin production of those exposed and to prevent DNA replication needed to restore damages. The result is a mutated or altered genetics which would be passed on to offsprings establishing a new norm generated by those exposed. Whereas they would have been black skinned initially, the alterations not only resulted in variations in the skin changes and less melanin production but was also passed on to any children given birth to. The process could be referred to as a micro-evolution where variations of the same is created. They are by no means so radically different as to be classified or categorized as being subspecies. The differences are only skin deep as only the skin tissue was sensitive to this ionized radiation. One can only imagine the number of deaths resulting from such exposure in the instances of skin cancer. However the presence of so-called 'white people' is testimony and a witnessing to the fact that many did survive having not received a lethal dosage. Subsequently a people who was at one time as black skinned as any dark or black skinned African who remained in Africa has a skin which has altered biochemistry producing less melanin except in the instance of its secondary system which can temporarily produce melanin given sufficient ultraviolet A, B exposure. Yet originally it was intended for the skin to produce an adequate amount of melanin continuously to keep the skin relatively dark. This was how the created humans started out. However environmental influences by being exposed caused these meaningless variations which are being abused and misrepresented and distorted for socio-political, economic and religious reasons being far from the created and/or scientific truth. It is clearly time that we face up to this and take on the concept of race as a disease needing to be eradicated along with any other terms conjured to divide humans.

Chapter Eight

To date all humans are failing to understand our blackness, treating it as a description of our differences. We witness the fact that the world has not only embraced the idea of race and polarized two skin colors, black and white, in extreme opposition but the idea has become institutionalized giving supposed matter of fact as a foundation for racism. Even those who do not fit neatly in one category or the other are being categorized as having a closer affinity to one or the other. Western thought and ideology has sought to limit the so-called Black race or African race to Negroid type to south of the Sahara desert. The efforts of many wanting to solidify such thinking having even gone so far as to say that any other black skinned people discovered elsewhere in the world were in fact to be described as little white men with dark skin such as the aborigines of Australia. It was suggested as being inconceivable that the Negroid African could have ventured out of Africa independent of any modern day conclusions of by captivity. Little did they know that these black skinned people such as the Australian aborigine were a testament to their own ancestors having been black. The aborigine were not little white men with black skin but rather they are descendants of migratory humans who had not lossed the ability to produce the necessary melanin needed for black skin.

Obviously such notions restricting the movement of the so-called Black people or African with Negroid features to within Africa south of the Sahara desert have been invalidated by and large within the scientific community. Race as a useful concept in describing people has been largely negated being a pseudo term. However this is not so within the every day world as we perceive it. Society still divides itself according to racial categories; local and world politics plays the race card; national and international economics is being driven by racism and conservative/fundamental religious practices have reacted and kept our churches mostly polarized along racial lines. Then there is a wedge being driven between individuals in education on account of race. There are people who do not even want certain people buried in the same cemetery as their deceased because of the color of one's skin.

The world has embraced the idea of race as a reality not because it has scientific proof because it does not being in fact to the contrary but rather because the idea of race had become institutionalized with black and white having become polarized.

While the concept of race existed by the 15th/16th centuries as people became more exposed to other people looking different from themselves, people began not only grouping themselves but attempting to give themselves a biological beginning such as lineage. The basis of this identity was usually some past remembered place of origin or was attributed to some past great ancestor. The true point of origin was long but forgotten. Hence people were establishing a history of origins based upon the context of the present situation where they had come to settle rather than in the context of where they had migrated from or originated. Their history was isogetical whereas they read into it that which was intended to bolster their identified group.

Subsequently any group separate from their own could be identified as a separate race of people with each group of people or race having their own point of origin based in some relatively recent but nearly forgotten historical event, person or family. The idea of race was being developed and institutionalized as suggesting something separate in Europe.

Yet they believed basically that all humans were essentially equal although believing their own group of people to have greater qualities. The use of race was intended primarily to provide a point of origin and a historical beginning. While this history may be significant, it is mythical with only some basis in fact. It fails to link all the human groups to one another. The history of this common ancestry of all humans has long since been forgotten as would have been the events resulting in irreversible hypopigmentation following the migrations of some human groups into environmental areas exposed to ionized radiation capable of skin color alterations.

For the most part because of environmental barriers and nearly insurmountable distances separating them, the people of these various groups would hardly have been aware of any developing phenotype differences. However as industrial expansion and population expansion with increase travel began, people became much more aware. Differences were being measured and categorized as well as defined through the spread of western ideology. Race would soon not only suggest a separate origin although having an assumed common ancestry biblically speaking. It would also take on the meaning which suggested demonstrable and measurable differences among human groups. It was thought that no only had humans branched out but in this branching out we somehow developed differently allowing some to be placed in one category and others in another lesser category. Each supposedly had distinctive racial qualities. This would become the lynchpin in the understanding of so-called human development. Some went so far as to refer to the development as evolution placing themselves at the top of the evolved human suggesting their own superiority. This is perhaps the beginning of institutionalized thinking as such thinking becomes manifest in every area of one's daily living, the perception that some people are different from one's self in categorical or racially defined terms. However as a M. Banton in The Idea of Race suggest:

"It is. . .unwise to study the idea of race in isolation from two other ideas that were likewise reborn in the early years of the nineteenth century. The modern ideas of race, of class, and of nation, arose from the same European milieu and share many points of similarity. All three were exported to the furthest parts of the globe and have flourished in many foreign soils. In so far as man have believed that it was right to align themselves on the basis of race, class, and nation, or have believed that these would become the major lines of division, so these ideas have proved their own justification."[1]

Such thinking has become a way of life with it being taken for granted. This is how things are suppose to be. This is how the system works and race has become part in total of this system. It has become institutionalized. We have established race as one of the foundations making it a basic premise of society. It is part of our educational character and is embodied like a thread through all areas of life involving human relations. We can see it in our school systems, the teachings at all levels, the religions, the economics, the segregated housing and in the day to day relations. "A Black man in San Diego recently received an apology from Radio Shack after he purchased an English-Spanish translator that he discovered used the translation 'nigger' for the word 'negro.'[2]

As race is primarily only used today in reference to obvious physical differences which have been categorized, the institutionalizing of race has focused on the polarization of colors, black versus white. Subsequently, "racism appears to be growing in America, retired U.S. Supreme Court Justice Harry A. Blackmun recently told a group of future lawyers. Nothing has yet convinced me that racism is not all about us, and at times seems to be growing stronger. . ."[3] Racism is all about us as part of the western ideological threads which weaves our societal structure as does class and nation. To extract it out will require some fundamental changes at the core of western thinking. A process which can occur if we are up to the task of reevaluating ourselves, all of us. Human morality and unity may depend upon this.

We will need to reconsider our traditional views which has given rise to doctrinal beliefs on the existence of not only differences believed to be real and significant on account of the idea, race, but on the existence of human racial categories believed to be permanent. M. Banton noted how President Abraham Lincoln believed "that there is a finite number of races or types (blacks and white being the most distant); that the differences are permanent; and that the differences have a decisive influence upon the kinds of social relationship possible between members of different races. . ."[4] The embracing of such doctrinal thoughts as printed "in a book called Types of Mankind which was published in Philadelphia in 1854"[5] drives home the point of such thinking becoming institutionalized. It was part of the system of how things are or are to be. Everyone has simply followed suit since with race becoming a factor in all facets of daily living and planning throughout the world.

Even when we claim to have surmounted the problems of using the term race, we find that we are really just denying or hiding our deeply embedded conscious beliefs on human groups being categorically different. "Notions of race having become so closely involved with the affairs of ethnic minorities that it is frequently unproductive to try to demarcate the study of race relations from the study of ethnic relations."[6] Even this concept of race being used to polarize humans on the basis of skin color can perhaps not be better stated than by President Abraham Lincoln "on the fourteeth of August 1862. . .:

You and we are different races. We have between us a
broader difference than exists between any other two

races. Whether it is right or wrong I need not discuss, but this physical difference is a great disadvantage to us both, as I think your race suffer very greatly, many of them by living among us, while ours suffer from your presence. . ."[7]

A group of so-called colored people was invited to the White House to be told of colored people's future plight by remaining in the United States. Society was clearly being established not only on the premise of national boundaries and class distinctions but that race was a reality in human deferences which could not be changed.

Given the image of one race being negative as a group, we can see why the perceived notions of one people being different from another are what they are. This imagery simply supports the status quo which is systematic or instituttionalized traditional beliefs with no basis in fact or truth. It is the belief which must be shaken as scientific understanding will not suffice to challenge closed and/or narrow minds who create their own pseudo science in efforts to establish and maintain an advantage.

We believe race to be at the core of our existence as witnessed in the statement by Lincoln. It is this understanding of race which has made racism so pervasive from being extinguished. It is the institutionalization of race as a basic premise in life that needs to be challenged in order to establish an understanding and format for its demise. At present as in the not too distant past, everyone is being oriented towards the acceptance of the idea of race even though it is now known that race used to categorize is a non-term and is nonapplicable to humans. However it is the elucidness of belief in the idea of race which has propped up race as an essential to understanding human existence nourishing the acts of racism. Nevertheless it is the institutionalization of race that is the basis of this core belief. Such beliefs are not simply drawn from thin air but rather are the result of some developing thinking or intent even if we are unconscious of it having taken place. The belief is so well embedded that we no longer consider its origin instead embracing or rejecting its affect in racism.

Yet it is the elusiveness of a belief in the idea of race which has propped up race as an essential to understanding human existence nourishing the acts of racism because we believe that there are measurable differences of significance. The institutionalization of race is the basis of this core belief. Just as we view God as a male, we view humans as being racially divided. This is basic or fundamental to western worldview having been promoted perhaps by notions of superiority.

"Racism is essentially a pretentious way of saying that 'I' belong to the Best People. For such a conviction it is the most gratifying formula that has ever been discovered, for neither my own unworthiness nor the accusations of others can ever dislodge me from my position - - a position which was determined in the womb of my mother at conception. It avoids all embarrassing questions about my conduct of life and nullifies all embarrassing claims by 'inferior' groups about their own achievements and ethical standards."[8]

It did not develop overnight. Hence we will find that the idea of race and the act of racism has more of a historical basis rather than a scientific one. A Peter Loewenberg in "The Psychology of Racism" states:

". . . racism in America has deep historical roots. A variety of factors—social, economic, political, and religious—have interacted over a period of almost 400 years to implant racial ideologies in the American culture and to imbed racism in our institutions."

But American racial prejudice can not be understood simply in economic, political and intellectual terms. Racism is also personal and social in origin. It must also be seen as a psychological function of the personality related to character structure, patterns of society, and adaptation to personal and social change."[9]

Loewenberg goes further in giving support to what I describe as part of the process in institutionalizing race making it a core belief.

"On the issue of race, American society offers a prescribed set of responses which are clearly communicated–consciously and unconsciously–to all who reach adulthood in that society.

Prejudice is learned behavior. It is the natural result of participation in social patterns of prejudice. . . This is one of the processes by which racial attitudes are passed from generation to generation.

The typical American community, North as well as South, implies Negro inferiority in its pattern of living. . . Patterns of socializing in church, home and recreation centers. . . The child assimilates these patterns of stratification and separation naturally, with no conscious effort.

A white child coming of age in this setting acquires prejudice as a matter of course by living in his environment and internalizing its values. It is not necessary to teach him any explicit ideology of racism. He has only to observe and participate in his world. . . By the time a white child hears for the first time that 'Negroes are not inferior,' it is usually too late. Even if he is intellectually convinced of their equality. . ."[10]

These racial attitudes have been passed down so many times over that one is no longer even aware of doing so any more. It is simply being taken for granted that the concept of race is a legitimate one and we all believe it and constantly refer to it when dealing with those who appear different. I would contend that the issue of race has indeed been institutionalized.

While we may not fully understand the racism being prompted through the concepts of race, it is certain that we can examine ourselves in view of the prejudices we may harbour on account of the idea of race.

"A famous study, by T.W. Adorno and his associates,

The Authoritarian Personality, found that the primary feature of the racially prejudice personality is authoritarianism–a preoccupation with issues of power such as who is strong and who is weak. The study used questionnaires, in-depth interviews, and projective tests. The central finding is that prejudiced attitudes express inner needs. The authoritarian individual is a weak and dependent person who lacks the capacity for genuine experience of himself or others. Behind his facade of strength lurks a shaky sense of order and safety. His world is one of rigidly stereotyped categories of power, success, and punitive moralism. He seeks to align himself with the conventional, and with what is regarded by others as good and strong. But these are not his own values. He has underlying feelings of weakness and self-contempt which he suppresses and projects onto ethnic minorities and other out-groups. The authoritarian thinks in rigid categories of dominance and submission, those who command and those who obey, masters and slaves. For him weakness is contemptuous. It is associated with guilt. His identification with those in power is a reaction to deep feelings of inadequacy and weakness. He acts the role of the 'tough guy,' trying to appear hypermasculine, while in reality he has strong feminine dependent tendencies that he denies. His conceptions of masculinity and femininity are exaggerated and rigid. Therefore he fears and rejects all that appears as soft, feminine, or weak. . .

There follows a projections of all sinful, aggressive, and sexual impulses on outgroups and condemnation of these groups because of this projection."[11]

We must remember that in the context of racial prejudices. The tendency towards an authoritarian personality is dependent upon the active application of race as a legitimate idea and biological reality for use in describing individuals and/or groups of humans. Thus it is certain that in the instance of its use as pertains to race, this power is without foundation because no race can dominate over another if the concept of race is invalid. No one group is superior to another even though one may think so. The image of hypermasculinity seen in television commercials like the one with the Marlboro cigarette and the claim of authority/ superiority over others' humanity is a facade.

Whether or not we concern ourselves with the issue of authoritarian personalities, we must agree that not everyone who is prejudice is necessarily to be classified as such. Yet the institutionalizing of a belief in race and the fostering of racism continues. One primary reason appears to be the mass media with it expanding communications technology in the hand of those who subscribe to this notion of power as defined earlier. It begins with its efforts to always report matters from a majority or mainstream perspective. Rather than matter of fact reporting it tends to bait its audience with titillating descriptions and adjectives which are in tune with the racial attitude of society while simultaneously furthering or festering such ills in a society.

This imagery being given in various forms through mass media inevitably molds for us a model for human existence and interrelationship. The idea of race is being stimulated and facilitated by this means. This is not to say that it is guilty of some intentional ploy but rather to emphasize that it is a part of this institutionalizing of race. We believe it is so because the media said so. If not today, then it will tomorrow repeatedly always with an unmistakably racial slant to suggest separation and differences among humans. If this model of race is not being shown before us by the television, it is being heard on the radio, read in the print media or is being displayed in advertisement remaining ever present before us. It is even before us in idol conversation. We have to only internalized the concept of race but we perceive each race as it is portrayed before us time and time again by the mass media which is acting in behalf of a dominant or mainstream society who again believes in the idea of race.

"A study by Hartmann and Husband (1971) argues per-

suasively that the British mass media, including television, handle race relations material in a way that both perpetuates negative perceptions of blacks and also defines the race relations situation as one of intergroup conflict. . .the press treats race relations in terms of conflict, threat and deviance."[12]
Attempts to describe the million man march for atonement is just one such example where efforts were made to classify the march according to the controversial image having been given to the caller to discredit its potential for success. It should be emphasized that these negative perceptions and words suggesting intergroup conflict appear to be used primarily in relations to those other than the so-called white race being used particularly when reference is given of the so-called African American individual or group involvement. Again the problem with this imagery concerning race is universal. The example cited above very well could have been an occurence any where world-wide and in any situation where race is a factor. Even where the African or African American race is predominate such factors will still be evident because of this notion of the superiority of one race over the other. The so-called Black race appears to measure itself against the notion of a superior race with success being measured in how well one can immulate their characteristics.

This is perhaps no more apparent than in the large Black Churches although this notion of superiority has kept the Church as one of the most segregated institutions in existence today. Although such religious institutions may espouse equality among the so-called races, again, we are looking at traditional beliefs which have been institutionalized. We believe ourselves to be different according to race. Subsequently white churches embrace a white Jesus while many black churches have trouble embracing a black Jesus because of this superiority notion of white over black. Furthermore while so-called majority white church dominations are on record as having adopted statements or resolutions favoring integration to resolve the race problem as a church issue, "there is little evidence that the local white churches are as yet taking seriously the resolutions and pronouncements of their respective official bodies."[13] Yet it should not surprise us when "the more involved, more devoted Christians were also the most conservative on a variety of topics, ranging from political choices through toleration of political deviants to attitudes toward race."[14] A.C. Bagley states: "It appears that individuals who are committed to racialist attitudes are committed to a number of 'conservative' items.[15] Conservative like authoritarian is meant to imply that one has a racial prejudice. As concerns the church, we see this race consciousness, this racial prejudice in our beliefs. This suggest that race is fundamental to western society and ideology into which the religion of Christianity has been acculturated.

We live in a society which has been riddled with pseudo-imagery concerning race so much so that it has affected everything we do from our religious belief to our work and school relationships; from our political to our economic application. Subsequently, it has spawn multiple but misleading avenues for injecting images concerning pseudo concepts of race. Hence they become code words to perpetuate the same (race) knowingly or unknowingly such words as: ethnicity, conservative (suggesting status quo), minority in the context of race, fundamental, mainstream, etc. Race has become a functional image believed to be relevant to human understanding and as such becomes a model as perceived by the pseudo notions, descriptions/definitions surrounding it.

It has become institutionalized and universalized through this unyielding perception dating back to an error prone explanation of our biological differences. Time has served only to make this pseudo definition and its perception more insidious to resolution.

"Perception is the larger process of making meaningful sense out of sensation. . .

. . .in order for perception to occur the brain must

construct models. . . In any case, the brain must construct and store models so that it can later compare them with new receptor activity. . . It is these models that complete people's interfaces with their environments.

What I here called 'models' have been called by other names especially by the name 'schema.' Neisser provides the following description of a schema:
> A schema is that portion of the entire perceptual cycle which is internal to the perceiver, modifiable by experience, and somehow specific to what is being perceived. . .

The idea here is that we may sense the world more or less directly, but we perceive in a meaningful way our own models or schemata of things we sense. . . What we perceive is our own model.

When we look at something we seem to see it as it exists, in its essential entirety; but we really see in a psychologically usable way that which we expect, or (with somewhat greater delay) one of the expectable alternatives."[16]

The perception of there being an innate biological difference between humans of various geographical locations while being in error has remained both a prominent and permanent notion even up to now despite scientific disclaimers in the usage of race to categorize humans. It should be noted that such perceptions have and continue to arouse unjustifiable disturbing emotions from the need to dominate over groups deemed different from one's own to feeling of being superior to the other group; and from hate to murder/genocide to eliminate those groups believed to be different.

In other words these perceived notions have culminated into institutionalized models of whose imagery is relevant to the racism in today's society. Certain images have been formulated having been reinforced through the misrepresentation of science. This began with the Darwinian discussion on evolution which would discredit in large part the Christian biblical teachings on the creation of Adam and Eve from whom all other humans had come implying only one human race. Such thinking was to be challenged by this emerging theory on evolution with its so-called scientific truth regarding human development. P. Curtain in The Image of Africa states:

"For Darwinians, both polygenesis and mongenesis were beside the point, but racists could use the theory of natural selection to 'prove' that human varieties must be vastly different from one another. For monogenist, not only was the scientific basis for their position swept away, its other support in the authority of Christian revelation was no more valid for Darwinians than other aspects of the Christian tradition–when that tradition was confronted by scientific truth.

Meanwhile, in the last pre-Darwinian decades, as the racist position grew progressively stronger, the change was mainly one of degree: where earlier writers had held that race was an important influence on human culture, the new generation saw race as the crucial determinant, not only of culture but of human character and of all history. Hundreds of variant theories were to appear in the mood of this new emphasis. Some would claim the rigor of historical law, conceived in detail and projected into the future. Others were content to use the fact of race as a key to understanding the present condition of man. In either case, the basic theories were followed in turn by countless specific applications, special formulations, calls to action, warning of danger, and racio-political policies adopted by governments.

In time, the new racism was to become the most important cluster of ideas in British imperial theory. . . Racial differences, seen in black and white, were the natural place to begin. . .the new emphasis on race inevitably came to affect European attitudes towards the Africans."[17]

"With the growth of pseudo-scientific racism, much the same kind of bias could be introduced in the portrayal of facial features. . . Nor was this point left to the readers imagination."[18]
Efforts have been made to have history substantiate one's racial claims. History has served merely as a tool in establishing one's identity such as one's racial identity. "The discourse of attributing a meaningful past to a structured present. An objectivist history is produced in the context of a certain kind of selfhood, one that is based on a radical separation of the subject from any particular identity, and which objectifies and textualizes reality. . . This in turn leads to a truth-value representation of the past that is implicitly intolerant of anything that appears to distort the historical record 'as it really happened.'"[19] The historical record of Columbus discovering America is one such example. History can be isogetical in that one can read into it that which will benefit self or one's race to stand out among others. Just as Europeans have used history to construct an identity, the African American has used Africa to construct theirs. "Greece played a pivotal role as the place of origin of everything specifically Western, from science to democracy."[20] For some reason which is beyond me, it does not matter where Greece got its influence. All that matters is that one be linked to something or some past which allows one to stand out as being separate and special. "History, then, is very much a mythical construction, in the sense that it is a representation of the past linked to the establishment of an identity in the present. . .definition of self by means of the other."[21] "Although such history is not all true, European history has become an 'institutional memory.'"[22] Likewise Black Studies courses and/or seminars seek to make African history an institutional memory for the African American. In both instances it has been about proving one's race

for purposes of separating and standing out. Subsequently I close this chapter with following quote of J. Friedman:

"If history is largely mythical, it is because the politics of identity consists in anchoring the present in a viable past. The past is, thus, constructed according to the conditions and desires of those who produce historical texts in the present. This is as true of our own history as of anyone else's."[23]

Conclusion

This intent of writing has not been to simply state the problem. We already know that, the idea of Race. Further more it is not my intent to offer a solution but merely to point us in a particular direction. I am hopeful that this writing will serve to initiate a nation wide to world wide probing discussion and resolutions which in short order will conclude the idea of race to have been not only a mistake of the past but a divisive tool with inappropriate application then, in the present and for the future. Curiously we have sought to divide rather than to unite having a quest for political dominance over others deemed different while speaking simultaneously of God's love for all. Then it is unfortunate that some believe that God loves them more on account of a belief in race. Yet we use science and history even religion in a self serving effort to prove this. When in point of fact, the division of humanity has been an arbitrary effort of some to separate one's self or group from others.

With the development of western civilization, one appears to have engaged in the supremacy of human ideas over the ideas intended in God's creation that all humans are equal. It has been politics versus theology when one seeks to categorize humanity into races. The development of western society has been a tool of division and dominance ever since its beginning. Although it is merely an ideology demonstrating human effort to organize, politics has become the basis of our physical reality although through veiled eyes. Not only does one use it in seeking control over this physical reality but they are willing to sacrifice lives and factual scientific truths for this veiled idea. Such efforts have resulted in the institutionalization of the pseudo-scientific term, race. In other words, this racial division has merely been a pawn of the political will and ideas of a society. In fact were the factor of skin color removed, I fear that we would still engage in a reviving of racial categorization using other characteristics deemed distinctive and different amongst us. In such a case scenario even the United States would continue to experience racism if all African Americans disappeared as blond hair, blue eyes would challenge those with red hair and freckles. African American (Black) people have served more or less as a buffer preventing or limiting the focus on such divisions which are arguably as much a racial characteristic as is skin color. It may sound ridiculous but then so does black skin versus white skin because some pseudo definition said we are different when we really are not.

Then it is not so much whether or not it is true or real. It is more a question of what one believes to be real or true for purposes of constructing a self identity. This has been in large part the European Cosmology in an effort to give the idea of Western Civilization an ancestral foundation separate from all others. This western society has been created and institutionalized as a history to memory. We refer to it as European history for whites and African Americans have responded in like western fashion with an African Cosomology of our own putting us both in error. "The common understanding of history, peculiar to modern Western society, is one that consists in a stream of events, a temporal continuum whose empirical existence in unquestionable . . . It is. . .necessary to point out that exercises in the desconstruction of events that turn out, on closer examination, to be heavily interpreted. . .demonstrate the degree to which they are integral parts of the way in which we forge and reinforce our own identity.

"The establishment of a particular history was the work of identity construction, both for Europe and for Greece as an emergent periphery in the European world system. . .

These concerns of the cultural elites of Europe as well as those of their Mediterranean vassals formed the selective environment for the particular version of Greek history that was destined to become official.

If history is largely mythical, it is because the politics of identity consists in anchoring the present in a viable past. The past is, thus, constructed according to the conditions and desires of those who produce historical texts in the present. This is as true of our own history as of anyone else's."[1]

In other words European Cosmology could just as well have adopted an African temporal continuum for its ancestral foundation were it not for the pseudo determination of differences based on skin color. Of course they did not understand long ago given the immaturity of science but we do understand now. Yet this idea of race remains as a devisable term having been maintained for destruction and purposes of false human division. Does politics in fact rule over scientific reality and theological reflections or are we choosing to intentionally live a lie of human categorizing living in a world of persuasive deceit? The sins of a world society may lie in the refusal to know. If race is a pseudo term, then let us deal effectively with it and all associate words, thoughts and ideas. Racism can be eliminated.

One can not defeat racism with suggestions of equality and equal opportunity while yet legitimizing the idea of racial types because of the psyche and images which prevail that we are different biologically, mentally, and socially. This is why we keep failing so miserably. In our short sightedness, we have failed even to realize that this status quo support for the concept of race is a rather recently developed idea. It is not really that old having emerged basically as an institutional term in the early nineteenth century. It is now time that we look back again although not in the context of the present simply to give one self identity or to affirm the status quo but to determine rather the temporal continuum of humanity without subjecting it to political orientations.

We are much more alike than this contextualized history would intentionally permit one to say. According to a R. Lewontin:

"During the last forty years, using the techniques of immunology and of protein chemistry, it has been possible to identify a large number of human genes that codes for specific enzymes and other proteins. Very large numbers of individuals from all over the world have been tested to determine their genetic constitution with respect to such proteins, since only a small sample of blood is needed to make these determinations. About 150 different genetically coded proteins have been examined, and the results are very illuminating for our understanding of human genetic variation.

It turns out that 75 percent of the different kinds of proteins are identical in all individuals tested from whatever population, with the exception of an occasional rare mutation. These so-called monomorphic proteins are common to all human beings of all races, and the species is essentially uniform with respect to the genes that code them. The other 25 percent are polymorphic proteins. . ."[2]

"A major finding from the study of such polymorphic genes is that none of these genes perfectly discriminates one 'racial' group from another. That is, there is no gene known that is 100 percent of one form in one race and 100 percent of a different form in some other race. Reciprocally, some genes that are very variable from individual to individual show no average difference at all between major races.

Rather than picking out genes that are the most different or the most similar between groups, what do we see if we pick genes at random? . . .In this random sample of genes there is a remarkable similarity between groups. ...the most common form of each gene in Africans is the same form as for the Europeans, and the proportions themselves are very close. Such a result would lead us to conclude that the genetic difference between blacks and whites is negligible as compared with the polymorphism within each group."[3]

"The result of the study of genetic variation is in sharp contrast with the everyday impression that major 'races' are well differentiated. Clearly, those superficial differences in hair form, skin colour, and facial features that are used to distinguish 'races' from each other are not typical of human genes in general. Human 'racial' differentiation is, indeed, only skin-deep. Any use of racial categories must take its justification from some source other than biology."[4]

The efforts to contextualize history in the present and to institutionalize differences (race) has been an unmistakable error of the western society in its intent to dominate as seen in the colonizations, enslavement and oppression of others based on racial distinctions. Not only has western society sought to tame science for such use but it has used history and has resulted in others seeking to stake their own claims in history by doing likewise furthering the error.

Still, we can certainly learn from our past but we can not go back to relive it nor seek to hold it static for status quo using the excuse of tradition. If history is a temporal continuum, it continues to expand. It would be akin to a rooted tree with a large trunk and many large and many small branches. We have a past and a future but the present can not be seen clearly when viewed only in the context of one branch without viewing the entire tree with its many growing branches. We must view the entire human family without giving more importance to one segment. We are all merely branches of common parents. It would behoove us to remember this when being lured or tempted by contextualized history and ideas of racial division.

Despite the visible human variations, we remain genetically linked with mutated variations having been experienced superficially in our physical features, skin color and blood but not in one's human self intellectually or in one's spiritual relationship with the one God. Hence I refer us all back to the scripture Genesis 1:27

"So God created humankind in his image,
in the image of God he created them,
male and female he created them."

Neither gender is to be considered first nor either one superior to the other. Likewise, so are all humans the same in relations to one another in God's view. We are all variations of black which was God's intended creation. This fact has not changed. Nor does it matter how much we have, how much we know or how much we do not have and do not know. In fact we will find that as one nears death possessions, knowledge, gender nor skin color really seems to matter because they are only peripheral concerns of a social consciousness which we have artificially constructed.

Nevertheless having understood this, integration and/or assimilation has never been the social solution or remedy to this human dilemma of separation when the concept of race in and of itself clearly implies that there are categorical differences negating the potential to be viewed as equals. To date it has only resulted in each group or so-called race seeking to contextualize a history to give one's self and group stature and to measure one's self along side the so-called white race seeking its acceptance and recog-

122

nition. It is perhaps that we need to pursue education to quench everyone's ignorance to the invalidation of the concept race. However the effectiveness of such an effort may be meaningless if one fails to attack the institutionalization of race. Race has been deemed matter of fact and has become a basic core belief of all humans even those who know better. Then there are those individuals many perhaps both black and white who do not want things to change given their socio-economic-political status. Mass communications has become the tool of such individuals in not only perpetuating the idea of race but in causing so-called differences to be viewed as antagonistic facilitating/encouraging an environment of division.

"Through the selection and presentation of events as news, the media help establish and reaffirm the prevailing assumptions and values in the society. . ."[6] Mass media communications by and large has been used not only to promote race but the images and precepts associated with the concept. Mass media can be viewed as the standard bearer of political and social status quo. "The media (both entertainment and news) help to establish and reinforce the cultural boundaries within which our public discussion and thoughts about racial inequality occur. . ."[7] "What is presented and omitted from the news implicitly establishes (and reinforces) perceptions of the appropriateness and naturalness of the existing, moral , political, and racial order. The news media tend to support (through their selections, framing, omissions, and presentation) groups, institutions, and activities that embrace and maintain the enduring values of the society–capitalism, assimilation, individualism, and social order."[8] Race is a part of the social order and that social reality seemingly continued because of this communications both visual and auditory. These communications establish the imagery by which we consciously and unconsciously define ourselves and our relationship with others. This racial imagery is one of tension, conflict and differences.

Research has shown the media to be primarily a tool of

the so-called dominate society as it seeks to meet the needs of the consumer (those with purchasing power) and to ignore the concerns of others. Then where it does address the concerns of others, it does so only within the boundaries of cultural restraints which seek to keep status quo. We will find this in any news report, commercial or television program whether it be oriented towards African Americans or not because of the economic purse-strings of a dominate culture. Subsequently racial division has always been depicted either explicitly or subtly.

In fact it has been suggested that the idea of race has been driven by and large by economic greed and the need to remain politically dominate. Subsequently we live in someone's socio-political reality and not the physical reality of what is because race is merely a social concept and not a real or scientific validation of humans. In that the mass media along with its imagery has been solicited and captured as the domain of this socio-political reality, we the whole world wide out of misinformation accept it as factual whatever it presents because of the supposed credibility of the mass media to report truthfully and accurately. We can not ignore its impact upon a society. Where it is not for the power of the media's imagery, perhaps the idea of race would have gone the route of the dinosaur and would have become merely a reflection of our past ignorance on human blackness. After all what other sources have we to rely which offers such consistency in reporting and which virtually can shape for most what it is we think, do, or say.

Yet the mass media is not a value free operations. The intent of objectivity is more an ideal than an actuality in practice. As a result of human input, facts become artifacts having been subjected to one's social biases. Mass media must appease big business to gain those advertising dollars. Subsequently mass media needs to remain primarily conservative which is to say that it perpetuates status quo. This status quo means maintaining the idea of race and all of its associated language as a part of the conservative/traditional social reality and societal beliefs.

124

We can never succeed in racial equality until we view race as meaning one human race and not a categorization of humans. The mass media will need to become desensitized to color because of the power in the imagery being shown. It must cease portraying negative images for one and positive images for another. To date it has been unable to do so because of the controlling interest of big business and government to keep things as is for their benefit. Hence discussions and resolutions leading to the decomposition of the institution of race needs to begin not with the reporting of such imagery but with those responsible for creating and facilitating the imagery for self again. As such let the discussion and resolution begin in the corporate board rooms of big business, with the board of governors at the universities and colleges, with the board of education and school superintendents to actuate an effective program, in the congress and the president's cabinet, at the state and city government levels, as well as at the country clubs and the classroom. The idea of race must be edited out of human society because it is no longer and really never was applicable to human understanding. We could say that it was a rush to judgement in the past but the facts are in now and we need to talk about eradicating this concept of race and all associated language once and forever. Then we need a good public relations campaign in all areas of life to begin working on it.

A strong public relations campaign is needed to alter public opinion not only about the illegitimacy of race but to alter opinions about those deemed to be at the bottom of this make believe racial scale. For centuries we have been painting ourselves into a corner through mass media and political propaganda exploiting the pseudo-scientific concept of race. We must restore human value over the social factors which facilitates the development of cognitive processing resulting in stereotyping and a social identity. This understanding has contributed towards group formations and self categorization.

Such racial stereotyping has resulted in intergroup development and in intragroup comparison and conflict. As long as this stereotyping is in place, it does not matter what improvements a group/race makes in regards to the accusations or descriptions assigned to them by the other group. Stereotypes are modified as the situation warrants to keep things as they are. Thus an out group can always be identified or perceived as being different. The intergroup or many of the various members seek to sustain their group's relations. ". . .stereotype change is a product of specific alterations in intergroup relations. As a corollary where relations over time are characterized by stability, there is little or no change in stereotype content. With regard to this point, Fishman (1950) argued that if, as he claimed, stereotypes serve to reflect or rationalize intergroup relations, then it is unreasonable to expect them to change where all other elements of the relations between groups are unaltered."[9] The social context which has brought about a change in self identity from coloured to Negro to Black and now for many African-American supports the point made above. Circumstances regarding the gains made in self recognition and categorization has been met by modifications in the stereotyping because we are still viewed as the out group but only differently now. We are still being stereotyped within the social context of the status quo having been developed around the concept of race.

We are exposed to this stereotyping by "the news profession's dominant culture perception of daily events."[10] This has all the ear markings of stereotyping with one clearly being identified as the in-group. They (black or white) engage in 'preferred meaning' which 'have the whole social order embedded in them as a set of meanings, practices and beliefs: the everyday knowledge of social structures, of 'how things work for all practical purposes in this culture,' the rank order of power and interest and the structure of legitimation, limits, sanctions. . ."[11] We see the increasing employment of preferred meanings as regards the concept of race through the use of a "surrogate term,"[12] ethnic/ethnicity. (The idea was to replace the concept of race because of its "problematic baggage"[13]).

126

"From the mid-1930s the validity of race as a scientific concept was increasingly challenged by liberal South African academics. In 1936 the psychologist, I.D. MacCrone, attacked the dogmas of innate mental or racial capacity as unscientific. Citing the work of anthropologists like Bronislaw Malinowski and Margaret Mead, MacCrone suggested that the idea of 'group differences' should be substituted for the 'problem of race differences.' Such differences, he argued, ought to be analyzed in cultural or psycho-social terms by looking at attitudes and behavior.[7] Some years later, MacCrone extended this critique and echoing the suggestion of Huxley and Haddon in We Europeans, advocated banishing the word 'race' in favour of 'some such phrase as 'ethnic cultural' to describe those groups in which biological and cultural groups differences coincide with one another.'[8]"[14]

"In 1943, the social anthropologist, Hilde Kuper, delivered a telling attack on common 'racial myths'. . . Kuper argued that whites, blacks and coloureds were all part of the same species and that there was no scientific evidence that physical differences had any bearing on culture whatsoever. In her effort to divorce the notion of culture from race, Kuper slipped in the term 'ethnic' as an alternative–though without explanation or definition.[9]"[15]

The problem with the use of a surrogate term is explained later by S. Dubow:
"Biological notions of race were not necessarily repudiated; rather they were incorporated within a form of cultural essentialism that encouraged the articulation of human difference without explicit recourse to arguments based on biological determinism. In this context, the idea of ethnicity, combining a sense of primordial affiliation, biological descent, and cultural identity, was easily understood and internalised.[17]"[16]

This is why we must not only extricate the concept of race but all associated terms and language which can be used in the formation of intragroups on the basis of physical differences which are merely variations of the same.

While surrogate terms like ethnic/ethnicity are being substituted in order to sustain the formation of intragroups and the stereotyping of blacks, it should also be noted "that there is no single European or white race of man."[17] All so-called white people contrary to belief do not look alike but have significant physical difference as seen in black versus white. In fact there are sufficient arbitrary variations in their physical characteristics for a separate grouping or categorizing of Europeans suggesting the existence of multiple races in Europe. While society utilizes a preferred meaning which allows Europeans to be viewed collectively as one people, there is no such thing as a Caucasian race (Indo-Germanic or Indo-European) nor a Negroid or a Mongoloid race. Instead there are mulitple separate groups with distinct differences/variations. At least three so-called races have been identified in Europe. The arbitrary physical characteristics being used for these racial categorizations are: head and face shape, hair color, eye color, stature (height and body build) and, nose shape (skin color is obviously absent). The three races identified are the Teutonic, the Alpine (Celtic) and the Mediterranean. There is no one all inclusive superior white race (the Aryans). Interestingly enough many of those physical characteristics being used to identify these three so-called European races can be identified likewise within the so-called Negroid or African race suggesting that we are merely looking at variations in human physical characteristics and not racial distinctions and differences. These variations are the result of environmental influences. Such as measurable arbitrary variations have even been shown to exist in India and Turkey (both of whom have considered such variations mistakenly for possible racial distinction among their people) not to mention the continent of Africa. However these differences are to be viewed as human variations within one human species. All humans

128

are and have remained a black-skinned people. This fact can not be denied no matter what variations may be evident in one's skin color or physical characteristics.

The concept of race is an invalid term by which to divide humanity and has developed into a long term menacing and disruptive social disease having no biological support. Yet it can be remedied in short order given a commitment of the whole society and world keeping in mind that a substitute or surrogate term simply delays looking at this very real problem, the idea of race, and allows for a band aide solution which benefits and appeases a few while deceiving most into keeping things really the same. We should understand by now that this is the effort of a few not just for economic and political gain but for the right to shape and determine the future. While no future should be solidified without the full participation of all human groups, simply stated the idea of race, a pseudo-science, used the world over prevents this reality.

"One of the greatest enemies of science is pseudo-science. In a scientific age, prejudice and passion seek to clothe themselves in a garb of scientific respectability; and when they cannot find support from true science, they invent a pseudo-science to justify themselves. We all know that the Devil can quote Scripture for his own purpose: to-day we are finding that he can even invent a false Scripture from which to quote.

Nowhere is this lamentable state of affairs more pronounced than in regard to 'race.' A vast pseudo-science of 'racial biology' has been erected which serves to justify political ambitions, economic ends, social grudges, class prejudices."[18]

We must constantly remind ourselves that no one group is capable of determining the directions of human development singularly. We must all participate in the human destiny. We must not only get along but become the one human family which we are instead of collective, integrated groups in a hierarchical status. There must be a truly equal playing field for all because no one is better than the other nor does any one group deserve more opportunities or freedom than the other. There are no racial barriers. It is perhaps that we will begin to understand this when we realize that the human is more than the summation of one's physical possessions and designated status/titles, more than the summation of one's physical capabilities or intelligence. It is this that we must seek to know if we are to appreciate one another. So, if we truly care to get it right about this human equation, we must begin by telling the truth about the singularity of the human family. There is no black, white, red, yellow races only one biologically black-skinned humanity. Hence support of separate racial identity is folly from either side of the equation. Race is a nonsensical concept as regards humanity. The truth lies in viewing humanity as one with variations. Science knows this and now it is time that the world's societies came up to speed.

Notes

INTRODUCTION: A SOCIAL INVENTION

1. Rose L.H. Finkenstaedt, Face to Face: Blacks In America: White Perceptions And Black Realities (New York: William Marrow and Co. Inc., 1994) pp. 21.
2. R.C. Lewontin, "The Apportionment of Human Diversity," Evolutionary Biology Volume 6 (New York: Appleton-Century-Crofts, 1972) pp. 397.
3. Ibid. pp. 381.
4. P.A. Riley, "Mechanistic Aspects of the Control of Tyrosinase Activity," Pigment Cell Research Volume 6, no. 4, Part 1 (August 1993) pp.182.
5. Peter A von Rippel, David G. Bear, Robert O. Winter, Otto G. Berg, "Molecular Aspects of Promoter Function - An Overview," Promoters-Structure and Function (New York: Praeger Publisher, 1982) pp. 4.

1. RACE: A SOCIAL OR BIOLOGICAL TERM

1. "Race," Random House Unabridged Dictionary (2nd edition, printed 1993).

2. "Race," The New Caxton Encyclopedia (volume 16, 1979).
3. "Race," Encyclopedia Britannica (volume 18, 1973).
4. "Race," Academic American Encyclopedia (1989).
5. "Race," Chamber's Encyclopedia New Edition (volume XI, 1964).

2. ANTHROPOLOGY: ITS MISUSE IN CATEGORIZING HUMANS

1. David E. Hunter and Phillip Whitten, Encyclopedia of Anthropology (New York: Harper and Row Publisher, 1976), pp. 328.
2. R.C. Lewontin, "The Apportionment of Human Diversity," in Evolutionary Biology 6, ed. Theodosius Dobzhensky, Maas K. Hecht, William C. Steere (New York: Appleton - Century - Crofts, 1972), pp. 381.
3. David E. Hunter and Phillip Whitten, Encyclopedia of Anthropology (New York: Harper and Row Publisher, 1976), pp. 328.
4. Ibid., pp. 328.
5. Ibid., pp. 326.
6. "White Man Who Altered Himself To Look Black Reveals Chilling Accounts of Racism, Oppression," Jet (December 26 - January 2, 1995), pp. 26-27.
7. Ibid., pp. 26-27.
8. David E. Hunter and Phillip Whitten, Encyclopedia of Anthropology (New York: Harper and Row Publisher, 1976), pp. 184.
9. Ibid., pp. 184.
10. Joel S. Kahn, "Culture - Demise Or Resurrection?," Critique of Anthropology 9, no. 2 (Autumn, 1989), pp. 7.
11. Terence Turner, "Anthropology and Multiculturalism: What Is Anthropology That Mulitculturalists Should be Mindful of It?", Cultural Anthropology 8, no. 4 (November, 1993), pp. 411-412.

3. SCIENTIFIC RACISM: THE MAKING OF A PSEUDO-SCIENCE

1. Reading In Early Anthropology, ed. J.S. Slotkin, (New York: Wenner-Gren Foundation For Anthropological Research, Inc., 1965), pp. X.
2. Ibid., pp.X
3. Ibid., pp. X.
4. Elazar Barkan, "The Retreat of Scientific Racism," (Cambridge: Cambridge University Press, 1992), pp. 15.
5. Ibid., pp. 2.
6. Charles Leslie, "Scientific Racism: Reflections on Peer Review Science and Ideology," Social Science and Medicine 31, no. 8 (Newark, Deleware: Center for Science and Culture University of Deleware, 1990), pp. 897.
7. Ibid., pp. 899.
8. Ibid., pp. 899.
9. Ibid., pp. 900.
10. Roger Pearson, Ph.D.., Anthropological Glossary, The Institute for the Study of Man, Washington, D.C., (Malabar, Florida: Robert E. Krieger Publishing Co., 1985), pp. 218.
11. Encyclopedia of Anthropology, ed., David E. Hunter and Phillip Whitten, (New York: Harper and Row Publisher, 1976), pp. 326.
12. R.C. Lewontin, "The Apportionment of Human Diversity," Evolutionary Biology 6, ed., Theodosius Dobzkansky, Maus K. Hecht, William C. Steere, (New York: Appleton - Country - Crafts Publisher, 1972), pp. 397.
13. Susan Smith, "Preamble: on 'Race,' Residence and Segregation," The Politics of 'Race' and Residence, Susan Smith, (New York: Polity Press, 1989), pp. 3.
14. Gordon W. Allport, "The Nature of Prejudices," (Cambridge: Addison-Wesley Publishing Co., 1954), pp. 20-23.
15. S.L. Washburn, "The Study of Race," American Anthropologist 65, (1963), pp. 503, 523.

4. THE CYCLES OF RACISM IN AMERICA

1. Von Bakanic, "I'm not Prejudiced, But. . .: A Deeper Look at Racial Attitudes," Sociological Inquiry 65, no. 1, (Feb. 1995), pp. 67-86.
2. Ibid., pp. 67.
3. Reference Library of Black America 1, Compiled and ed.. Harry A. Ploski and James Williams, (New York: Afro-American Press, 1980), pp. 111.
4. Ibid., pp. 16
5. Ibid., pp. 16-17.
6. Encyclopedia of African American Civil Rights, ed., Charles D. Lowery and John F. Marszalek, (New York: Greenwood Press, 1992) pp. 202.
7. Ibid., pp. 50.
8. Reference Library of Black America 1, Compiled and ed., Harry A. Ploski and James Williams, (New York: Afro-American Press, 1980), pp. 17.
9. Ibid., pp. 17.
10. Ibid., pp. 17.
11. Ibid., pp. 17.
12. Ibid., pp. 17-18.
13. Ibid., pp. 18.
14. Ibid., pp. 18.
15. Ibid., pp. 18.
16. Ibid., pp. 18.
17. Ibid., pp. 18.
18. Ibid., pp. 18.
19. Ibid., pp. 18.
20. Ibid., pp. 18-19.
21. Ibid., pp. 19.
22. Ibid., pp. 19.
23. Ibid., pp. 19.
24. Ibid., pp. 19.
25. Ibid., pp. 19.
26. Ibid., pp. 20.
27. Ibid., pp. 20.
28. Ibid., pp. 21.

29. Ibid., pp. 21.
30. Ibid., pp. 23.
31. Ibid., pp. 23.
32. Ibid., pp. 23.
33. Ibid., pp. 23.
34. Ibid., pp. 26.
35. Ibid., pp. 26.
36. Ibid., pp. 28.
37. Ibid., pp. 28-29.
38. Ibid., pp. 29.
39. Ibid., pp. 29.
40. Ibid., pp. 30.
41. Ibid., pp. 30.
42. Ibid., pp. 30.
43. Ibid., pp. 30.
44. Ibid., pp. 30.
45. Ibid., pp. 32.
46. Ibid., pp. 32.
47. Donald E. Muir, "Race: The Mythic Roots of Racism," Sociological Inquiry 63, no. 3, (August, 1993), pp. 339-350.

5. BIOLOGICAL RESPONSE TO ENVIRONMENTAL CHANGE

1. John H. Relethford, "Craniometric Variation Among Modern Human Populations," American Journal of Physical Anthropology 95, no. 1, (Sept. 1994), pp. 53-54.
2. Eric Czable and Richard Handler and Anna Lawson, "On the Uses of Relativism: Fact, Conjecture and Black and White Histories at Colonial Williamsburg," American Ethnologist 19, no. 4, (Nov., 1992), pp. 791-792.
3. Chapter One "The Framework of Migration Studies," Biological Aspects of Human Migration, ed., C.G.N. Mascie-Taylor, G.W. Lasker, (Cambridge: Cambridge Press, 1988), pp, 1.
4. Ibid., pp. 2.
5. Ibid., pp. 2.

6. Ibid., pp. 3.
7. Ibid., pp. 3-4.
8. Ibid., pp. 4.
9. John H. Relethford, "Craniometric Variation Among Modern Human Populations," American Journal of Physical Anthropology, 95, no. 1, (Sept., 1994), pp. 53.
10. Ibid., pp. 53-54.
11. Biological Aspect of Human Migration, ed. C.G.N. Mascie-Taylor, G.W. Lasker, (Cambridge: Cambridge Press, 1988), pp. 12.
12. Ibid., pp. 130-131.
13. Jonathan Marks, "Blood Will Tell (Won't It?): A Century of Molecular Discourse on Anthropological Systematics," American Journal of Physical Anthropology, 94, no. 1 (May, 1994), pp. 63.
14. Ibid., pp. 63.
15. Kenneth La Beals and Courtland L. Smith and A.J. Kelso, "ABO Phenotype and Morphology," Current Anthropology, 33, no. 2, (April, 1992), pp. 222.

6. ALL HUMANS ARE BIOLOGICALLY BLACK

1. Ashley H. Robins, Biological Perspective on Human Pigmentation, (Cambridge: Cambridge University Press, 1991), pp. 1.
2. Ibid., pp. 3.
3. Ibid., pp. 14.
4. Ibid., pp. 12.
5. Ibid., pp. 17.
6. Ibid., pp. 12.
7. Ibid., pp. 15.
8. Ibid., pp. 17.
9. Ibid., pp. 60.
10. Ibid., pp. 25.
11. Ibid., pp. 30.
12. William Montagna, Ginseppe Prota, John A. Kenney, Jr., "Black Skin Structure and Function," (San Diego:

Acdemic Press, Inc. a Division of Harcourt Brace and Co., 1993), pp. 22.

13. Ibid., pp. 53.
14. Ibid., pp. 31.
15. Ibid., pp. 37.
16. Ibid., pp. 37.
17. Ibid., pp. 38.
18. Ibid., pp. 38.
19. Ibid., pp. 54.
20. Ibid., pp. 96.
21. Ibid., pp. 95.
22. Ashley Robins, "Biological Perspectives On Human Pigmentation," (Cambridge: Cambridge University Press, 1991), pp. 62.
23. William Montagna, Ginseppe Prota, John A. Kenney, Jr., "Black Skin Structure and Function," (San Diego: Academic Press, Inc. a Division of Harcourt Brace and Co., 1993), pp. 72.
24. Ibid., pp. 12.
25. Victor Arena, "Ionizing Radiation and Life," (St. Louis: The C.V. Mosby Co., 1971), pp. 371.
26. P.A. Riley, "Mechanistic Aspects of the Control of Tyrosinase Activity," 6, no. 4, (August, 1993), pp. 182.
27. Kazunori Urabe, Pilar Aroca, and Vincent J. Hearing, "From Gene to Protein = Determination of Melanin Synthesis," Pigment Cell Research, 6, no. 4, (August, 1993), pp. 186.
28. Ibid., pp. 188.
29. Daniel S. Grosch and Larry E. Hopwood, "Biological Effects of Radiation," (New York: Academic Press, 1979), pp. 5.
30. Ibid., pp. 66.
31. Walter Harm, "Biological Effects of Ultraviolet Radiation," (Cambridge; Cambridge University Press, 1980), pp. 142.
32. Daniel S. Grosch and Larry E. Hopewood, "Biological Effects of Radiation," (New York: Academic Press, 1979), pp. 66.

33. C.C. Berdjis, M.D., "Cell," Pathology of Irradiation, ed. Charles C. Berdjis, M.D., (Baltimore: The Williams and Wilkins Co., 1971), pp. 10-31.

7. CAUSES OF VARIATION IN HUMAN BLACKNESS

1. D.J.H. Brock, "The Structure and Function of Proteins: Effect of Mutation," The Biochemical Genetics of Man, ed. D.J.H. Brock and O. Mayo, (London and New York: Academic Press, 1978), pp. 31
2. Ibid., pp. 32.
3. Ibid., pp. 33.
4. "The Origins and Diversity of Human Populations," An Introduction to Human Genetics, 4th ed., H. Eldon Sutton, (San Diego and New York: Harcourt Brace Jovanavich Publisher, 1988), pp. 553.
5. Ibid., pp. 554.
6. "Mutations: Nature and Consequences," An Introduction to Human Genetics, 4th ed., H. Eldon Sutton, (San Diego and New York: Harcourt Brace Jovanavich Publisher, 1988), pp. 248.
7. William Montagna, Giuseppe Prota, John A. Kenney, Jr., Black Skin Structure and Function, (San Diego: Academic Press, 1984), p. 72.
8. A.K.E. Gustafsson, Cold Spring Harbor Symposia On Quantitative Biology vol. XVI, (Long Island, New York: The Biological Laboratory Cold Spring Arbor, 1951), p. 278.
9. Daniel S. Grosch and Larry E. Hopwood, Biological Effects of Radiations, (New York: Academic Press, 1979), p.9.
10. "Mutations: Nature and Consequences," An Introduction to Human Genetics, 4th ed. H. Eldon Sutton, (San Diego and New York: Harcourt Bruce Jovanavich Publisher, 1988), p. 258.
11. Malcolm Dole, "Introduction," The Radiation Chemistry of Macromolecules, ed. Malcolm Dole, vol. 1, (New York: Academic Press, 19), p. 3.

12. Daniel S. Grosch and Larry E. Hopwood, Biological Effects of Radiations, (New York: Academic Press, 1979), p. 66.
13. Ibid., p. 17.
14. Ibid., p. 66.
15. C.F. Tessmer, "Radiation Effects in Skin," Pathology of Irradiation, ed. Charles C. Berdjijs, (Baltimore: The Williams and Wilkins Co., 1971), p. 150.
16. Thomas K. Gaisser, Cosmic Rays and Particle Physics, (Cambridge: Cambridge University Press, 1990), p. 90-91.
17. Pierre Sokolsky, Introduction to Ultrahigh Energy Cosmic Ray Physics, (Redwood, California: Addison - Wesley Publishing Co. Inc., 1989), p. 9.
18. Thomas K. Gaisser, Cosmic Rays and Particle Physics, (Cambridge: Cambridge University Press, 1990), p. 91.
19. Millard F. Coffin and Olan Eldholm, "Large Igneous Provinces," Scientific American, vol. 269, no. 4 (October, 1993), p. 42.
20. Rene Gallant, "Radio - Activity," Bombarded Earth, Rene Gallant, (London: John Baker Publishing Ltd., 1904), p.156.
21. Ibid., p. 176.
22. Ibid., p. 177, 178.
23. Robert T. Rood, Craig L. Sarazin, Edward J. Zeller, and Brace C. Parker, "X or Y-rays from Supernovae in Glacial Ice," Nature, vol. 282, no. 5740, (13 December, 1979), p. 701.
24. Ibid., p. 701.
25. M. Ruderman and J.W. Truran, "Possible Transfer of Lunar Matter to Earth Due to a Nearby Supernova," Nature vol. 284, no. 5754, (27 March, 1980), p. 328.
26. Ibid., p. 328.
27. M.A. Ruderman, "Possible Consequences of Nearby Supernova Explosions for Atmospheric Ozone and Terrestial Life," Science, vol. 84, no. 4141, (7 June, 1974), p 1080.

8. THE PERPETUATION OF RACE
AS AN INSTITUTION

1. Michael Benton, The Idea of Race, (Boulder, Co.: Westview Press, 1978), p. 3.
2. "Radio Shack Apologizes for Selling Device Offensive to Black Customer," Jet, vol. 88, no. 9, (July 10, 1995), p. 52.
3. "Former Justice Blackman Says Racism Is Growing," Jet, vol. 88, no. 6, (June 19, 1995), p. 32.
4. Michael Benton, The Idea of Race, (Boulder, Co.: Westview Press, 1978), p. 5.
5. Ibid., p. 5.
6. Ibid., p. 8.
7. Ibid., p. 1.
8. Ruth Benedict, Race: Science and Politics, Revised ed. with The Races of Mankind, Ruth Benedict and Gene Weltfish, 1943, (New York: The Viking Press, 1949), p. 99.
9. Peter Loewenberg, "The Psychology of Racism," The Greater Fear: Race In the Minds of America, ed. Gary B. Nash, Richard Weiss, (New York: Holt, Rinehardt and Winston, 1970), p. 186.
10. Ibid., p. 187.
11. Ibid., p. 196.
12. Christopher Bagley and Gajendra K. Verna, "The Mass Media as Agents in the Development and Support of Prejudice and Discrimination," Racial Prejudice: The Individual and Society, (Great Britain: Saxon House, 1979), p. 164.
13. John C. Leggett, "The Uneven Impact of Institutions: The University and the Church," Race, Class and Political Consciousness, (Cambridge: Schenkman Publishing Co., Inc., 1972), p. 112.
14. Ibid., p. 113.
15. Christopher Bagley, "Racial Prejudice and the 'Conservative' Personality: A British Sample." Political Studies, vol. XVIII, no. 1, (March, 1970), p. 141.

16. Eric Klinger, "The Central Place of Imagery in Human Functioning," Imagery Vol. 2, Concepts, Results, and Applications, ed. Eric Klinger, (New York and London: Plenum Press, 1980), p. 4-5.
17. Philip D. Curtin, "British Ideas and Action 1780 - 1850," The Image of Africa, (Madison: The University of Wisconsin Press, 1964), p. 363-364.
18. Ibid., p. 366.
19. Jonathan Friedman, "Myth, History, and Political Identity," Cultural Anthropology, vol. 7, no. 2, (May, 1992), p. 194.
20. Ibid., p. 195.
21. Ibid., p. 195.
22. Ibid., p. 206.
23. Ibid., p. 207.

CONCLUSION. RIDDING SOCIETY OF THE NONSENSICAL TERM RACE

1. Jonathan Friedman, "Myth, History, and Political Identity," Cultural Anthropology, vol. 7, no. 2, (May, 1992), p. 206-207.
2. Richard Lewontin, "Are The Races Different?", Anti-Racist Science Teaching, ed. Dawn Gill and Less Levidow, (London: Free Association Books, 1987), p. 201-202.
3. Ibid., p. 203-205.
4. Ibid., p. 207.
5. Genesis 1:27, Old Testament, Bible.
6. Herman Gray, "Race Relations As News," American Behavioral Scientist, vol. 30, no. 4, (March/April, 1987), p. 381.
7. Ibid., p. 383.
8. Ibid., p. 388.
9. S. Alexander Haslam, John C. Turner, Penelope J. Oakes, Craig McCarty, and Brett K. Hayes, "Context - Dependent Variation in Social Stereotyping 1: Effects of Intergroup Relations As Mediated By Social Change

and Frame of Reference," European Journal of Social Psychology, vol. 22, no. 1, (January-February, 1992), p. 6.

10. Christopher Campbell, Race, Myth and the News, (London: Sage Publication, 1995), p. 3.
11. Ibid., p. 2.
12. Saul Dubow, "Ethnic Euphenism and Racial Echoes," Journal of Southern African Studies, vol. 20, no. 3, (September, 1994), p. 356.
13. Leonard Lieberman and Fatimah Linda C. Jackson, "Race and Three Models of Human Origin," American Anthropologist, vol. 97, no. 2, (June, 1995), p. 233.
14. Saul Dubow, "Ethnic Euphenism and Racial Echoes," Journal of Southern African Studies, vol. 20, no. 3, (September, 1994), p. 356.
15. Ibid., p. 357-358.
16. Ibid., p. 359.
17. William Z. Ripley, The Races of Europe: A Sociological Study, (New York: D. Appleton and Co., 1899 and New York: Johnson Reprint Corp., 1965), p. 103.
18. Julian Huxley and A.C. Haddon, We Europeans: A Survey of Racial Problems, (London: J. Cape, 1935), p. 7.

Bibliography

Aharoni, Yohanan, The Archaeology of the Land of Israel, Miriam Aharoni, ed; Anson F. Rainey, translator, Philadelphia: The Westminister Press, 1982.

Allen, Richard L.; Dawson, Michael C.; Brown, Ronald E.; "A Schema-Based Approach To Modeling An African-American Racial Belief System," American Political Science Review, 83, no. 2, (June 1989), pp. 421-441.

Allport, Gordon W., The Nature of Prejudices, Cambridge: Addison - Wesley Publishing Co., 1954.

Arena, Victor, Ionizing Radiation And Life, St. Louis: The C.V. Mosby Co., 1971.

Bagdikian, Ben H., The Media Monopoly, Boston: Beacon Press, 1983.

Bagley, Christopher, "Racial Prejudice and the 'Conservative' Personality: A British Sample," Political Studies, XVIII, no. 1, Oxford: Clarendon Press, (March, 1970).

Bagley, Christopher and Verna, Gajendra K., "The Mass Media as Agents in the Development and Support of Prejudice and Discrimination," Racial Prejudice: the

Individual and Society, Great Britain: Saxon House, 1979.

Bahn, Paul G., "Outdoor Creations of the Ice Age," Archaeology, 48, no. 4, (July/August, 1995) pp. 37.

Bakanic, Von, "I'm Not Prejudiced, But. . ." A Deeper Look at Racial Attitudes," Sociological Inquiry, 65, no. 1, (February, 1995), pp. 67-86.

Banton, Michael, The Idea of Race, Boulder: Westview Press, 1978.

Barkan, Elazar, The Retreat of Scientific Racism, Cambridge: Cambridge University Press, 1992.

Baskin, Wade and Runes, Richard N., "Slave: Though 20 negroes were sold in Jamestown, Virginia, in 1619, the word 'slave' was not used in Virignia to designate negroes until 1662." Dictionary of Black Culture, New York: Philosophical Library, 1973, pp. 405.

Bastide, Roger, "Color, Racism, and Christianity," Daedalus - Journal of the American Academy of Arts and Science, 96, 1967, pp. 312-327.

Beals, Kenneth L.; Smith, Courtland L.; and Kelso, A.J., "ABO Phenetype and Morphology," Current Anthropology, 33, no. 2, (April, 1992), pp. 221-224.

Benedict, Ruth, Race: Science and Politics, Revised ed. with The Races of Mankind, Ruth Benedict and Gene Weltfish, 1943, New York: The Viking Press, 1949.

Berdjis, Charles C., "Cell," Pathology of Irradiation, ed. Charles C. Berdjis, Baltimore: The Williams and Wilkins Co., 1971, pp. 19-31.

Bethlehem, Douglas W., A Social Psychology of Prejudice, London and Sydney: Croom Helm, 1985, pp. 77-99.

Biddiss, Michael D., "The Racial Theory," Father of Racist Ideology: The Social and Political Thought of Count Godineau, New York: Weybright and Talley, 1970, pp. 112-121.

Bogdanor, Vernon, ed., The Blackwell Encyclopedia of Political Science, Cambridge: Blackwell Publishers, 1991.

Bouzek, Jan, "Climatic Changes: New Archaeological Evidence From the Bohemian Karst and Other Areas," Antiquity, 67, no. 255, (June, 1993), pp. 386-393.

Brace, C. Loring and Hunt, Kevin D., "A Nonracial Craniofacial Perspective on Human Variation: A(ustralia) to Z(uni)," American Journal of Physical Anthropology, 82, no. 3, (July, 1990), pp. 341-360.

Brace, C. Loring, "The Roots of the Race Concept in American Physical Anthropology," A History of American Physical Anthropology 1930 - 1980, ed. Frank Spencer, New York: Academic Press, 1982, pp. 11-29 and 412-443.

Brock, D.J.H., "Chapter One: The Structure and Function of Proteins," and "Chapter Five: Effects of Mutation," The Biochemical Genetics of Man, ed. D.J.H. Brock and O. Mayo, London and New York: Academic Press, 1978.

Cable, Joanne; Jackson, Ian J.; and Steel, Karen P., "Light (B^{lt}), a Mutation That Causes Melanocyte Death, Affects Stria Vascularis Function in the Mouse Inner Ear," Pigment Cell Research, 6, no. 4, (August, 1993), pp. 215-225.

Campbell, Christopher P., Race, Myth, and The News, London and New Delhi: Sage Publication, 1995.

Canning, Albert S.G., Literary Influence In British History, London: T. Fisher Unwin, 1904.

Casson, Ronald W., "Discussion and Criticism: On Brightness and Color Categories: Additional Data," Current Anthropology, 33, no. 4, (August - October, 1992), pp. 395-399.

Caucian, Francesca M., "Truth and Goodness: Does the Sociology of Inequality Promote Social Betterment?", Sociological Perspectives, 38, no. 3, (1995), pp. 339-356.

Chase, Philip G., "What Were the Ice Ages?", Expedition, 34, no. 3, (1992), pp. 4-13.

Chen, Yu - Sheng; Torroni, Antonio; Excoffier, Laurent; Santachiara - Benerecetti, A. Silvana; and Wallace, Douglas C., "Analysis of mt DNA Variation in African

Populations Reveals the Most Ancient of All Human Continent - Specific Haplogroups," American Journal of Human Genetics, 57, (1995), pp. 133-149.

Clark, D.H.; McCrea, W.H.; and Stephenson, F.R., "Frequency of Nearby Supernovae and Climatic and Biological Catastrophes," Nature, 265, no. 5592, (January 27, 1977), pp. 318-319.

Clube, Victor and Napier, Bill, The Cosmic Winter, Cambridge: Basil Blackwell, inc., 1990, pp. 237-243.

Coffin, Millard F. and Eldholm, Olan, "Large Igneous Provinces," Scientific American, 269, no. 4, (October, 1993), pp. 42-49.

Colman, Andrew M. and Lambley, Peter, "Authoritarianism and Race Attitudes In South Africa," The Journal of Social Psychology, 82, (December, 1970), pp. 161-164.

Cox, Diane W., "Genes of the Copper Pathway," The American Journal of Human Genetics, 56, no. 4, (April, 1995), pp. 828-834.

Curtin, Philip D., "British Ideas and Action 1780-1850," The Image of Africa, Madison: The University of Wisconsin Press, 1964.

Czable, Eric; Handler, Richard; and Lawson, Anna, "On the Uses of Relativism: Fact, Conjecture and Black and White Histories at Colonial Williamsburg," American Ethnologist, 19, no. 4, (November, 1992), pp. 791-792.

Dole, Malcolm, The Radiation Chemistry of Macromolecule, ed. Malcolm Sole, 1, New York: Academic Press, 1972.

Dorman, L.I., Cosmic Rays - Variation and Space Explorations, North Holland Publishing Co., 1974.

Dubinin, Nikolai Petrovich, Problems of Radiation Genetics, translated by G.H. Beale, Edinburgh: Oliver and Boyd, 1964.

Dubow, Saul, "Ethnic Euphemisms and Racial Echoes," Journal of Southern African Studies, 20, no. 3, (September, 1994), pp. 355-370.

Duckitt, John, "Conformity to Social Pressure and Racial

Prejudice Among White South Africans," Genetics,
Social, and General Psychology Monographs, 120, no.
2, (May, 1994), pp. 123-143.

Duckitt, John, "Right - Wing Authoritarianism Among White
South African Students: Its Measurement and Corre-
lates," The Journal of Social Psychology, 133, no. 4,
(August, 1993), pp. 553-563.

Elliot, G.A. and Tyson, G.A., "The Effects of Modifying Color
- Meaning Concepts on the Racial Attitudes of Black
and White South African Preschool Children," The Journal of Social Psychology, 121, no. 2, (December, 1983),
pp. 181-190.

Finkenstaedt, Rose L.H., Face to Face: Blacks In America:
White Perceptions and Black Realities, New York: William Marrow and Co. Inc., 1994.

Flexner, Stuart Berg, ed. in chief, "race," Random House
Unabridged Dictionary, 2nd ed., New York: Random
House inc., 1993, pp. 1590.

Foner, Philip S., "National Independent Political Union February 1876 'Negro Declaration of Independence,'" We:
the Other People: Alternative Declaration of Independence by Labor Groups, Farmers, Women's Rights
Advocates, Socialists, and Blacks, Philip S. Foner, ed.,
Urbana: University of Illinois Press, 1976.

Fontana, Josep and Colin - Smith, Troby, The Distorted Past
- A Reinterpretation of Europe, Oxford and Cambridge:
Blackwell, 1995.

Friedman, Jonathan, "Myth, History, and Political Identity,"
Cultural Anthropology, 7, no. 2, (May, 1992), pp. 144-210.

Gaisser, Thomas K., "Cosmic Rays," Cosmic Rays and Particle Physics, Cambridge: Cambridge University Press,
1990.

Gallant, Rene, "Radio - Activity," Bombarded Earth, London: John Baker Publishing Ltd., 1904.

Gibbs, David N., "Political Parties and International Rela-
tions: The United States and the Decolnization of Sub-
Saharan Africa," The International History Review,
XVII, no. 2, (May, 1995), pp. 221-440.

Gill, Dawn and Levidow, Les, ed., Anti-Racist Science Teaching, London: Free Association Books, 1987.

Goodall, Brian, "Race," The Facts On File: Dictionary of Human Geography, New York: Facts on File Publications, 1987.

Gray, Herman, "Race Relations As News," American Behavioral Scientist, 30, no. 4 (March/April, 1987), pp. 381-396.

Greenstein, Ran, "The Study of South Africa Society: Towards A New Agenda For Comparative Historical Inquiry," Journal of South African Studies, 20, no. 4, (December, 1994), pp. 641-661.

Greenstock, C.L. and Trivedi, A., Progress in Biophysics and Molecular Biology, 61, no. 2, 1994, pp. 104-106.

Grosch, Daniel S. and Hopwood, Larry E., Biological Effects of Radiations, New York: Academic Press, 1979.

Gross, Alan G., The Rhetoric of Science, Cambridge: Harvard University Press, 1990.

Gustafuan, AKE, "The Mutation Under Conditions Extreme or Adverse to the Mother Strain: Mutation, Environment and Evolution," Cold Spring Arbor Symposia on Quantitative Biology, XVI, Long Island: The Biological Laboratory Cold Spring Arbor, 1951, pp. 268-278.

Hallam, A., "The End of the Cretaceous," Nature, 281, no. 5731, (11 October, 1979), pp. 430-431.

Harm, Walter, Biological Effects of Ultraviolet Radiation, Cambridge: Cambridge University Press, 1980.

Hartmann, Paul and Husband, Charles, Racism and the Mass Media, New Jersey: Rowan, Littlefield, Totowa, 1974.

Haslam, S. Alexander; Turner, John C.; Oakes, Penelope J.; McGarty, Craig; and Hayes, Brett, "Context-Dependent Variation in Social Stereotyping 1: The Effects of Intergroup Relations as Mediated by Social Change and Frame of Reference," European Journal of Social Psychology, 22, no. 1, (January - February, 1992), pp. 3-20.

Hippel, Peter A. von; Bear, David G.; Winter, Robert O.; and Berg, Otto G.; "Molecular Aspects of Promoter

Function: An Overview," Promoters - Structure and Function, ed. Raymond L. Rodriguez and Michael J. Chamberlin, New York: Praeger Publisher, 1982.

Hob, Kafu, translator (Ewe), "A Baby Is A European," Poems From Africa, selected by Samuel Allen, 1973, pp. 42.

Holliday, Treton W. and Falsetti, Anthony B., "Lower Limb Length of European Early Modern Humans in Relation to Mobility and Climate," Journal of Human Evolution, 29, no. 2, (August, 1995), pp. 141-153.

Holub, Robert C., "After Realism: The Nonreflecting Mirror and the Unchanging Portrait," Reflections of Realism, Detroit: Wayne State University Press, 1991.

Holzmuller, Werner, "Information and Storage in Biological Systems," Information in Biological Systems: The Role of Macromolecules, translated by Manfred Hecker, Cambridge: Cambridge University Press, 1984, pp. 76-96.

Hornsby, Alton, Jr., Chronology of African American History, Detroit and London: Gale Research inc., 1991.

Hublin, Jean-Jacques, "The First Europeans," Archaeology, 49, no. 1, (January/February, 1996), pp. 36-44.

Hunter, David E. and Whitten, Phillip, ed. Encyclopedia of Anthropology, New York: Harper and Row, 1976.

Huxley, Julian S. and Haddon, A.C., We Europeans - A Survey of 'Racial' Problems, London: Jonathan Cape Publishing, 1935.

Jenkins, Richard, "Rethinking Ethnicity: Identity, Categorization and Power," Ethnic and Racial Studies, 17, no. 2, (April, 1994), pp. 197-223.

Jet, "Black Man Who Looks White Tells How He Struggled To Become Dean At Ohio State," 87, no. 17, (March 06, 1995), pp. 8.

Jet, "Former Justice Blackman Says Racism Is Growing," 83, no. 6, (June 19, 1995), pp. 32.

Jet, "Radio Shack Apologizes For Selling Device Offensive To Black Customer," 88, no. 9, (July 10, 1995), pp. 52.

Johnston, R.J.; Gregory, Derek; Smith, David M., eds.,

"race. . .The idea that human beings can be readily divided into a series of discrete 'races' is now widely regarded as fallacious: a political and social construction rather than a biological fact, the product of Racism rather than of human genetics." The Dictionary of Human Geography, 3rd ed., Oxford and Cambridge: Basil Blackwell, 1994.

Kahn, Joel S., "Culture: Demise or Resurrection?", Critique of Anthropology, 4, no. 2, (Autumn, 1989), pp. 5-25.

Keita, S.O.Y., "Further Studies of Crania From Ancient Northern Africa: An Analysis of Crania From First Dynasty Egyptian Tombs, Using Multiple Discriminant Functions," American Journal of Physical Anthropology, 87, no. 3, (March, 1992), pp. 245-254.

Kerns, Sharon E., "Transient - Ionization and Single-Event Phenomena," Ionizing Radiation Effects In MOS Devices and Circuits, T.R.M. and Paul V. Dressendorfer, eds., New York: John Wiley and Son, 1989, pp. 485-576.

Kligman, A. and Bahim, A.K., "Aging and the Human Skin," Aging and the Skin, New York: Raven Press, 1988.
["It is even more difficult to classify early hominids because paleontological findings are few and mostly fragmentary. Since it is very difficult to separate the single species of H. sapiens into its various races, all racial subdivisions of H. sapiens are arbitrary (Lasher 1961)." p. 13]

Klinger, Eric, "The Central Place of Imagery in Human Functioning," Imagery Volume 2: Concepts, Results and Applications, Eric Klinger, ed., New York and London: Plenum Press, 1980.

Krantz, Grover S., Climatic Races and Descent Groups, North Quincy, Massachusetts: The Christopher Publishing House, 1980.

Larick, Ray and Ciochon, Russell, "The First Asians," Archaeology, 49, no. 1 (January/February, 1996_, pp. 51-53.

Larsen, Knud S., "Race and Culture Courses: An Approach

to Attitude Change," Australian Institute of Aboriginal Studies. Newsletter, New Series, no. 8, (June, 1977), pp. 31-58

Leggett, John C., "The Uneven Impact of Institutions: The University and the Church," Race, Class and Political Consciousness, Cambridge: Schenkman Publishing Co., 1972.

Lemonick, Michael D., "How Man Began," Time, 143, no. 11, (March 14, 1994), pp. 80-87.

Leslie, Charlie, "Scientific Racism: Reflections On Peer Review, Science and Ideology," Social Science and Medicine, 31, no. 8, 1990, pp. 891-912.

Lewis, Marvin A., Afro-Hispanic Poetry 1940 - 1980: From Slavery to Negrotud In South American Verse, Columbia: University of Missouri Press, 1993, pp. 131-175.

Lewontin, Richard C., "Are The Races Different?", Anti-Racist Science Teaching, Dawn Gill and Les Levidow, eds., London: Free Association Books, 1987.

Lewontin, Richard C., "The Apportionment of Human Diversity," Evolutionary Biology, Theodosius Dobzhensky; Maas K. Hecht; William C. Steere, eds., volume 6, New York: Appleton - Century - Crofts, 1972, pp. 341-398.

Lieberman, Daniel E., "Testing Hypotheses - About Recent Human Evolution From Skulls," Current Anthropology, 36, no. 2, (April, 1995), pp. 159-197.

Lieberman, Leonard and Jackson, Fatimah Linda C., "Race and Three Models of Human Origin," American Anthropologist, 97, no. 2, (June, 1995), pp. 231-242.

Loewenberg, Peter, "The Psychology of Racism," The Greater Fear: Race In The Minds of America, Gary B. Nash and Richard Weiss, eds., New York: Holt, Rinehardt and Winston, 1970, pp. 186-201.

Lorcin, Patricia M.E., "Race and Scholarship in Algeria: The Impact of the Military," Imperial Identities: Stereotyping, Prejudice and Race in Colonial Algeria, London and New York: I.B. Taurus Publishers, 1995, pp.118-145.

Lorcin, Patricia M.E., "Scholarly Societies in France: the Kabyle Myth as a Racial Paradigm," Imperial Identities: Stereotyping, Prejudice and Race in Colonial Algeria, London and New York: I.B. Taurus Publishers, 1995, pp. 146-166.

Lorincz, Allan L., "Pigmentation," Physiology and Biochemistry of the Skin, Stephen Rothman, ed., Chicago: The University of Chicago Press, 1954, pp. 515-553.

Lowery, Charles D. and Marizalek, John F., ed., Encyclopedia of African-American Civil Rights, New York: Greenwood Press, 1992, pp. 50-51.

MacLaury, Robert E., "From Brightness to Hue: An Explanatory Model of Color-Category Evolution," Current Anthropology, 33, no. 2, (April, 1992), pp. 137-186.

Majumder, Partha; Shankar, B. Uma; Basu, Amitabha; Malhorta, Kailash C.; Gupta, Ranjan; Mukhopadhyay, Barun; Vijayumar, M.; and Roy, Subrata K., "Anthropometric Variation in India: A Statistical Appraisal," Current Anthropology, 31, no. 1, (February, 1990), pp. 94-103.

Malik, Kenan, "Universalism and Difference: Race and the Postmodernists," Race and Class, 37, no. 3, (January-March, 1996), pp. 1-17.

Markley, O.W., "Human Consciousness in Transformation," Evolution and Consciousness, Erich Jantsch and Conrad H. Waddington, eds., Reading: Addison-Wesley Publisher Co., 1976, pp. 214-229.

Marks, Jonathan, "Blood Will Tell (Won't It?): A Century of Molecular Discourse on Anthropological Systematics," American Journal of Physical Anthropology, 94, no. 6, (May, 1994), pp. 63.

Marshack, Alexander, "Images of the Ice Age," Archaeology, 48, no. (July/August, 1995), pp. 28-36 and 38-39.

McNeill, William H., "Mythistory or Truth, Myth, History, and Historians," Mythistory and Other Essays, Chicago and London: The University of Chicago Press, 1986.

Megarry, Jacquetta, ed., Education of Minorities, London: Kogan Page; New York: Nichols Publishing Co., 1981.

Mier, Paul D. and Cotton, W.K., "Pigmentation," The Molecular Biology of Skin, Oxford and London: Blackwell Scientific Publication, 1976, pp. 200-212.

Miller, Randall M. and Smith, John David, eds., Dictionary of Afro-American Slavery, New York: Greewood Press, 1988.

Montagna, William; Prota, Ginseppe; and Kenney, John A., Jr., Black Skin Structure and Function, San Diego: Academic Press, inc., 1993.

Montagna, William, "Skin: The Melanocyte Milieu," Pigmentation: Its Genesis and Biologic Control, Vernon Riley, ed., New York: Appleton - Century - Crofts, Meredith Corporation, 1972, pp. 1-22.

Mosse, George L., Toward the Final Solution: A History of European Racism, Madison: The University of Wisconsin Press, 1985.

Muir, Donald E., "Race: The Mythic Root of Racism," Sociological Inquiry, 63, no. 3, (Summer/August, 1993), pp. 338-350.

Murdock, Graham, "Large Corporations and the Control of the Communications Industries," Culture, Society and the Media, Michael Gurevitch; Tony Bennett; James Curran; and Janet Woollacott, New York: Mathneu, 1982, pp. 118-150.

Myers, L.S., Jr., "Radiation Chemistry of Nucleic Acids, Proteins, and Polysaacharides," The Radiation Chemistry of Macromolecules, Malcolm Dole, ed., New York: Academic Press, 1972, pp. 323-374.

Nash, Paul, Authority and Freedom in Education, New York: John Wiley and Saulaen, 1966.

Pearson, Roger, Anthropological Glossary, The Institute for the Study of Man, Washington, D.C. and Malabar, Florida: Robert E. Krieger Publishing Co., 1985, pp. 218-219.

Ploski, Harry A. and Williams, James, eds., "Chronology: A Historical Review," Reference Library of Black America Volume 1, Detroit: Afro-American Press, Gale Research, 1990.

Pollard, Ernest C., "Physical Considerations Influencing Radiation Response," The Biological Basis of Radiation Therapy, Emanuel E. Schwartz, ed., Philadelphia and Toronto: J.B. Lippincott Co., 1966, pp. 1-27.

Reish, Orit; Townsend, DeWayne; Poerry, Susan A.; Tsoi, Michael Y.; and King, Richard A., "Tyrosinase Inhibition Due to Interaction of Homocystinuria Due to Cystathionine B-Synthase Deficiency," American Journal of Human Genetics, 57, no. 1, 1995, pp. 127-132.

Relethford, John H., "Craniometric Variation Among Modern Human Populations," American Journal of Physical Anthropology, 95, no. 1, (September, 1994), pp. 53-54.

Riley, P.A., "Mechanistic Aspects of the Control of Tyrosinase Activity," Pigment Cell Research, 6, no. 4, Part 1, (August, 1993), pp. 182-185.

Ripley, William Z., "The Three European Races," The Races of Europe: A Sociological Study, New York: D. Appleton and Co., 1899, New York: Johnson Reprint Corp., 1965, pp. 103-130.

Roberfroid, Marcel and Calderon, Pedro Bue, Free Radicals and Oxidation Phenomena In Biological Systems, New York: Marcel Dakkar, Inc., 1995.

Robins, Ashley H., Biological Perspectives On Human Pigmentation, Cambridge: Cambridge University Press, 1991.

Robinson, James L., Racism or Attitude? - The Ongoing Struggle for Black Liberation and Self-Esteem, New York: Insight Books and Plenum Press, 1995.

Rockwell, Sara, "Radiobiology," Encyclopedia of Human Biology, 6, Renato Dulbecco, ed., San Diego and New York: Academic Press, Inc., 1991, pp. 441-453.

Roebrocks, Wil and Van, Thijs, "The Earliest Occupation of Europe: A Short Chronology," Antiquity, 68, no. 260, (September, 1994), pp. 489-503.

Rood, Robert T.; Sarazin, Craig L.; Zeller, Edward J.; and Parker, Bruce C., "X or Y-rays From Supernovae in

Glacial Ice," Nature, 282, no. 5740, (13 December, 1979), pp. 701-703.

Rothman, Stephen, Physiology and Biochemistry of the Skin, Chicago: University of Chicago Press, 1954.

Ruderman, M. and Truran, "Possible Transfer of Lunar Matter to Earth Due to a Nearby Supernova," Nature, 284, no. 5754, (27 March, 1980), pp. 328-329.

Ruderman, M.A., "Possible Consequences of Nearby Supernova Explosions for Atmospheric Ozone and Terrestial Life," Science, 84, no. 4141, (7 June, 1974), pp. 1079-1081.

Sahlins, Marshal, "Colors and Cultures," Semiotica, 16, no. 1, 1976, pp. 1-22. "The interesting implication of a semiotic theory of color categories, however, is that the mind-culture relation is more adequately conceived the other way around. The structures of the mind here appear not as the imperatives of culture but as its implements. They constitute a set of organizational means and possibilities at the disposition of the human cultural enterprize, which remains at liberty to variously engage them or not, and also to variously invest them with meaningful content. How else to account for the presence in culture of universal structures that are nevertheless not universally present? And at another level, how else to deal, other than mystically, with such contradictions in terms as 'collective consciousness,' 'collective representation,' or 'objectified thought,' which attribute to an entity that is social a function patently individual? To answer all questions of this kind, it will be necessary to situate the human mental equipment as the instrument of culture instead of the determinant. Then, like Hegel's cunning of Reason, the wisdom of the cultural process would consist in putting to the service of its own intentions natural systems which have their own reasons." pp. 18.

Sampson, Clavil Garth, The Stone Age Archaeology of Southern Africa, New York: Academic Press, 1974.

Sankaranarayanan, K., "Ionizing Radiation, Genetic Risk

Estimation and Molecular Biology: Impact and Infer-
ences," Trends in Genetics, 9, no. 3, (March, 1993),
pp. 79-84.

Sciara, Frank J., "Skin Color and College Students Prejudice," College Student Journal, 17, no. 4, (Winter,
1983), pp. 390-394.

Sertima, Ivan Van, "African Science Before The Birth of the
'New' World," The Black Collegian, 22, no. 3, (Janu-
ary/February, 1992), pp. 69-71.

Shibahara, Shigeki, "Mutations of the Tyrosinase Gene in
Oculocutaneous Albinism," Pigment Cell Research,
5, no. 5 (November, 1992), pp. 279-283.

Sinclair, Warren K. and Fry, R.J. Michael, "Mechanisms of
Radiation Interaction with DNA: Potential Implications
for Radiation Protection," Radiation Research, 112, no.
3, (December, 1987), pp. 407-417.

Slotkin, James Sydney, ed., Reading In Early Anthrolopogy,
New York: Wenner Gren Foundation For Anthropological Research, Inc., 1965.

Smith, Joseph, "Protection of the Human Race Against
Natural Hazards," Geology, 13, no. 10, (October,
1985), pp. 676.

Smith, Susan, ,"Preamble: on 'Race,' Residence and Segregation," The Politics of 'Race' and Residence, New
York: Polity Press, 1989, pp. 1-22.

Smolicz, J.J., "Culture, Ethnicity and Education:
Multiculturalism in a Plural Society," Education of Mi-
norities, Jacquetta Megarry; Stanley Nisbet; and Eric
Hoyle, ed., New York: Kogan Page and London:
Nichols Publishing Co., 1981, pp. 17-36.

Sokolsky, Pierre, Introduction to Ultrahigh Energy Cosmic
Ray Physics, Redmond City, California: Addison,
Wesley Publishing Co. Inc., 1989.

Straus, Lawrence Guy, "Southwestern Europe at the Last
Glacial Maximum," Current Anthropology, 32, no. 2,
(April, 1991), pp. 189-198.

Stringer, Christopher B., "New Views on Modern Human
Origins," The Origin and Evolution of Humans and

156

Humaness, D. Tab Rasmussen, ed., Boston: Jones and Bartlett, 1993.

Sturtvant, Alfred Harvey, A History of Genetics, New York: Haper and Row, 1965.

Sutton, H. Eldon, ed., "Mutations: Nature and Consequences," An Introduction to Human Genetics, San Diego and New York: Harcourt, Brace, Jovanovich Publishers, 1988.

Sutton, H. Eldon, ed., "The Origins and Diversity of Human Populations," An Introduction to Human Genetics, San Diego and New York: Harcourt, Bruce, Jovanovich Publishers, 1988.

Taylor, C.C.W., "A Note on Ancient Attitudes Towards Slavery," Analysis, 43, no. 1, (January, 1983), pp. 40.

Tessmer, C.F., "Radiation Effects in Skin," Pathology of Irradiation, Charles C. Berdjis, ed., Baltimore: The Williams and Wilkins Co., 1971, pp. 19-31.

Therman, Eeva, ed., "Causes of Chromosome Breaks," Human Chromosomes: Structures, Behavior, Effects, New York: Springer-Verlug, 1986.

Therman, Eeva, ed., "Chromosome Structural Aberrations," Human Chromosome: Structures, Behavior, Effects, New York: Springer - Verlug, 1986.

Therman, Eeva, ed., "The Action of Ionizing Radiation on the Heredity of Animals, Plants, Micro-Organisms and Viruses," Human Chromosomes: Structure, Behavior, Effects, New York: Springer - Verlug, 1986.

Turner, Terance, "Anthropology and Multiculturalism: What Is Anthropology That Multiculturalists Should be Mindful of It?", Cultural Anthropology, 8, no. 4, (November, 1993), pp. 411-412.

Ulin, Robert C., "Critical Anthropology Twenty Years Later," Critique of Anthropology, 11, no. 8, 1991, pp. 63-89.

Upton, Arthur C., "Pathologic Effects," The Biological Basis of Radiation Therapy, Emanual E. Schwartz, ed., Philadelphia and Toronto, 1966, pp. 126-162.

Urabe, Kazunori; Aroca, Pilar; and Hearing, Vincent J., "From

Gene to Protein: Determination of Melanin Synthesis," Pigment Cell Research, 6, no. 4, (August, 1993), pp. 186-192.

Vickerman, Milton D., "Race and Racial Groups," Survey of Social Science, 4, Frank N. Magul, ed., Pasadena, California and Englewood Cliffs, New Jersey: Salem Press, 1994, pp. 1552-1558.

Vincent, John J., "Education: Indoctrination or Enlightment?", The Race Race, London: SCM Press, LTD, 1970.

Voget, Fred W., A History of Ethnology, New York: Holt, Rinehart, Wiston, 1975.

Wallace, Steven P., "Racial Differences Among Users of Long Term Care," Research on Aging, 14, no. 4, (December, 1992), pp. 471-495.

Washburn, S.L., "The Study of Race," American Anthropologist, 65, 1963, pp. 503-531.

Watt, D.C.; Spencer, Frank; and Brown, Neville, A History of the World in the Twentieth Century, New York: William Morrow and Co., Inc., 1968, pp. 104-107 and 366-371.

Wax, Murray L., "How Culture Misdirects Multiculturalism," Anthropology and Education Quarterly, 24, no. 2, (June, 1993), pp. 99-113.

Weiss, Paul, Cinematics, Southern Illinois: Southern Illinois University Press, 1984.

Westhof, Eric, ed., "Water Structure," Water and Biological Macromolecules, London: The MacMillan Press, 1993, pp. 3-44.

Williams, John E., and Edwards, C. Drew, "An Exploratory Study of the Modification of Color and Racial Concept Attitudes in Preschool Children," Child Development, 40, no. 3, (September, 1969), pp. 737-750.

Woodward, Val, Human Hereditary and Society, St. Paul and New York: West Publishing Co., 1992., pp. 195-214.

Wysner, Glora M., The Kabyla People, Privately Printed, 1945.

If a social idea or equation is not congruent with its known biological true counter part and has historically been shown to be detrimental to the health and understanding of humankind, it is to be defined as a disease and methodology is to be developed for its eradication from society.

Race is one such idea being noncongruent with human biological skin coloring. Race is a social disease having no biological truth with which to support a belief in categorizing humans. Race is the social invention of a small segment of humanity being perpetuated and used to keep everyone ignorant of the blackness in human skin color.

To date race is what we believe or perceive it to be and not what it really is. An understanding of skin coloring can result in attitudinal changes. I challenge you to read this book and come away with the same views about race as before you completed the book. Then I challenge you to join me in helping to eradicate the term race and all of its social associates i.e. ethnic, minority, majority, etc.

"Historically, skin changes provided the first evidence of the biologically destructive nature of ionizing radiation." p. 146 (C.F. Tessmer, 1971)

159